FAVORITE RECIPES *of* NEW ENGLAND

FAVORITE RECIPES *of* NEW ENGLAND

PORTLAND HOUSE

CONTENTS

Edited and Introduced by Judith Ferguson
Photographed by Neil Sutherland
Designed by Philip Clucas
Coordinated by Hanni Penrose
Produced by Ted Smart, David Gibbon
and Gerald Hughes

CLB 1824
©1988 Colour Library Books Ltd., Guildford, Surrey, England.
All rights reserved.
Printed and bound in Hong Kong
Typeset by Words & Spaces, Hampshire, England
Published in 1988 by Portland House a division of dilithium Press, Ltd.,
Distributed by Crown Publishers, Inc. 225 Park Avenue South.
New York, New York 10003
ISBN 0 517 64529 7
h g f e d c b a

INTRODUCTION

Thickly forested mountains, thriving dairy farms, peaceful village greens, and wave-battered, rocky coasts – these are just a few of the images evoked by thoughts of New England. Steeped in history, yet with a firm eye on the future, this beautiful region is one of incredible contrasts: there are timeless old seaports and river towns as well as dynamic cities, majestic mansions, and modest salt-box houses. A sense of history pervades everyday life in New England. If we close our eyes we can almost see men in breeches and tricorn hats, and women in long, flowing capes living and working in colonial towns that have witnessed centuries of the nation's history.

As much as America progresses, we can still find evidence of our heritage if we look for it. This is never more evident than when we trace the roots of our culinary history. We learn from our earliest schooldays the important part food played in the colonization of the New World. The first settlers landed with stores of hardtack (hard biscuits), cheese, beer, and dried fish, which had sustained them on their voyage. Having endured this diet on their journey, they were anxious for fresh food, and found the abundance of clams, oysters, and mussels very welcome. They brought seeds for their crops with them from the Old World, but when these failed and starvation threatened, they discovered the bounty of the New World. The colonists found unusual foods that were destined to become staple crops and favorites of generations of Americans.

The native Indians introduced the colonists to maize, squash, tomatoes, and pumpkins. The newcomers learned about the wild turkey, which the Indians had succeeded in domesticating, and they were introduced to a true North American food – cranberries. These berries grew wild in the peat and sandy soil of Massachusetts and proved to be very versatile. The Indians used cranberries as a fabric dye and poultice for arrow wounds as well as for food. Pilgrim women soon discovered that cranberries brightened up a meal, and they began making sauces, pies, breads, and puddings with them. Thus was created the first Thanksgiving dinner – a celebration of hard work and survival. We still enjoy those same foods every year at Thanksgiving.

At first, the settlers used favorite recipes brought with them from home, adapting them to make use of ingredients available in the new land. The English side of our heritage gave us the recipes for meat pies and steamed puddings now found in our national fare. But other nationalities have made their contributions, too. One of the most American of dishes – clam chowder – is said to have French origins. French fishermen used to celebrate the safe return of the fleet by contributing a portion of the catch and cooking it right at the dock in large kettles – *chaudières* – from which the word chowder is derived. The fish was combined with salt pork, onions, potatoes, and milk to make a thick, creamy soup-stew that was a meal in itself. Since clams were cheap, plentiful, and obtainable without going to sea, many variations evolved from these dockside soups.

No one knows how tomatoes first slipped into clam chowder, but New Englanders will tell you that they don't belong there! A fierce controversy has raged for at least a century over the use of tomatoes in clam chowder. So seriously do New Englanders take the taste and appearance of one of their favorite soups that a bill was even introduced in one of the states' legislatures outlawing the use of tomatoes.

When talking of seafood, the discussion must also include another New England tradition – the clambake. The early settlers learned from the Indians how to dig for clams and how to steam them. The whole procedure must have seemed exotic indeed, but the result was delicious. Lobsters were first cooked in the same way, and while their flavor was appreciated, they were considered just an everyday food. Native to New England, the now highly prized North American lobster could, in the early days, be bought for a penny apiece, and people often apologized if that was all they could offer their guests to eat!

New England has contributed so many good things to America's culinary heritage. There is maple syrup – a real North American specialty and a natural sweetener used by the early settlers. There are Boston Baked Beans, which were frozen and then wrapped in cloth to take on journeys – the original "fast food." There are corn bread and blueberry muffins, delectable cakes and fruit pies, and, of course, the wonderful fish, such as bluefish and butterfish, that are indigenous to New England's waters.

Immigrants from many other countries soon joined the original settlers, and their influence is seen in dishes such as New England Pot Roast, which owes much to German *sauerbraten,* and New England Boiled Dinner, with its Irish origins. Yet these dishes, and many others with foreign connections, have evolved into representatives of true American cooking.

The evolution is still going on, and the best place to learn about the best in New England cooking is from the people who live and work there. We went along to find out. Come join us.

CONNECTICUT

Connecticut, meaning "place of the long river," was the name the Algonquin Indians gave to this area which became one of the original thirteen American colonies. It was a very appropriate name, for the first settlements were all established along the river banks as trading posts.

With its peaceful village greens, 17th- and 18th-century houses, steepled churches, old seaports and tree-lined country lanes, Connecticut has everything that symbolizes New England. With fertile and easily arable river valley land and a moderate climate, this was farming country almost exclusively until the early 19th century. The economy shifted once Eli Whitney developed a system for industrial mass production, but manufacturing never took over completely. Today, with an increasing interest in fresh, home-grown food, agriculture continues to be important to the state's economy.

Food in this part of New England reflects its traditional farming history. Like the recipe for the Grilled Vegetable Medley or various apple preparations such as Cider Mill Apple Dessert, Connecticut cuisine comprises good, wholesome fare based on local ingredients, and it is here that dishes such as Boiled New England Dinner and New England Pot Roast are still highly valued and very popular.

The main ingredient in a traditional Boiled New England Dinner is corned beef. Drying, smoking, and corning (or salting) of meat was the only way to keep it for use through the winter. The word "corned" had nothing to do with the American corn crop, as one might likely guess. The method – an ancient one – dates back to Anglo-Saxon Britain and a time when the type of salt used for curing meat had grains the size of a kernel of wheat – corn to these ancient Britons. The corning or salting process in colonial America followed a simple recipe:

> "For every hundred weight of beef use a peck of coarse salt, a half pound of salt peter, a quart of molasses, 2 pounds of coarse brown sugar, and pickling spice (usually a mixture of allspice berries, mustard seeds and bay leaves)."

The beef and salt were layered in a crock or barrel and left overnight. The following day the saltpeter, dissolved in some tepid water, was added to the molasses, or sugar and spices, and the whole was poured over the meat. Usually a board or some other weight was placed on the meat to keep it submerged in the brine. The meat was ready to eat after ten days, and was accompanied by cabbage, turnips, carrots, and potatoes. Along with cabbage, corned beef became a popular meal to celebrate St. Patrick's Day, as it reminded Irish immigrants of their favorite bacon and cabbage dish. Fortunately for us, corned beef is readily available without the time-consuming preparation.

New England (or Yankee) Pot Roast has been popular in Connecticut, and indeed all over the country, for well over two centuries. The dish can trace its ancestry to German *sauerbraten* and French *daube*. Add to this the influence of the Austrian and Russian immigrants in the 1840s and you have recipes as diverse as the country itself.

Recipes from Connecticut truly represent the culinary history of all the New England colonies. Corn and squash, two staple crops that were easy to grow and stored well, encouraged the development of recipes such as Corn Pudding and Butternut Squash Soup. Indian Pudding is a New England favorite that combines the English method for baked puddings with the produce of the New World. The curiously named Johnnycakes – cornmeal cakes – are still enjoyed, often with maple syrup.

No matter how innovative American cooks become (and the independent spirit does extend to the kitchen!), they always return to their old and much-loved favorites – the traditional dishes that are part of Connecticut's heritage.

Facing page: Butternut Squash Soup (top), Pea Soup (bottom left) and Cabbage Soup (bottom right).

CABBAGE SOUP

This is a quickly prepared soup with a very traditional country flavor.

Preparation Time: 20 minutes
Cooking Time: 45 minutes
Serves: 6

INGREDIENTS

1 small cabbage, finely chopped
½ a small onion, chopped
2 carrots, peeled and grated
Beef stock or 3 rounded tsps beef bouillon powder or
3 bouillon cubes

METHOD

Cook the cabbage, onion and carrots in the stock or bouillon with just enough water to cover. Cook about 45 minutes or until the vegetables are tender. Add salt and pepper to taste and serve.

MRS. MARY ROY,
DEAN'S MILL FARM,
STONINGTON, CT

PEA SOUP

Dried peas have been a staple food in this country since the first settlers set foot on dry land. Almost every country in the Western World has a recipe for pea soup, but the addition of a ham bone seems to be particularly American.

Preparation Time: 20 minutes
Cooking Time: 30-40 minutes
Serves: 6-8

INGREDIENTS

1 package split green peas (no soaking required)
1 tbsp grated onion
1 stalk celery, thinly sliced
1 carrot, peeled and thinly sliced
1 ham bone with some meat attached

METHOD

Pick over the split peas and add them to a large pot along with all the other ingredients. Cover with water and cook for 30-40 minutes, adding more water if needed. Remove the bone from the soup, take off the meat and chop it finely. Return the meat to the soup and serve with parsley and crackers.

MRS. MARY ROY,
DEAN'S MILL FARM,
STONINGTON, CT

BUTTERNUT SQUASH SOUP

This soup is traditional New England fare. The flesh of the butternut squash is denser and meatier than other varieties, so it makes a rich, thick soup without any additional thickening.

Preparation Time: 25 minutes
Cooking Time: 30-45 minutes
Serves: 4-6

INGREDIENTS

1 butternut squash, peeled, seeds removed and cubed
1 onion, diced
1 apple, peeled, cored and sliced
2 chicken bouillon cubes
1½ cups milk
2 tbsps brown sugar
Pinch salt and pepper
2 tbsps butter

METHOD

Place the prepared squash in a large pot with the apple and half the onion. Pour in the bouillon, cover the pot and cook until the squash is just tender. Do not overcook. Melt the butter in a sauté pan and cook the remaining onion until translucent and golden in color. Strain the soup and reserve the liquid. Place the squash, apple and onion in a food processor and return to the pot. Do not overwork the mixture; it should be coarsely chopped. Add 1½ cups milk to the soup and reheat gently. Add the sautéed onion and the sugar and enough of the reserved liquid to bring the soup to a thick, creamy consistency.

DANIEL ROUTHIER,
DEAN'S MILL FARM,
STONINGTON, CT

Above: Skewered Seafood and Pork with Lime-Curry Marinade.

SKEWERED SEAFOOD AND PORK WITH LIME-CURRY MARINADE

These fish kabobs can be cooked under a preheated gas grill or over hot coals. The combination of fish and pork with a lime and curry marinade gives this barbecue food an Indonesian flavor.

Preparation Time: 25 minutes
Cooking Time: 8-10 minutes
Serves: 4

INGREDIENTS

8 large sea scallops
8 large shrimp, shelled, leaving the end of the tail on if desired
½lb thick sliced roast pork
¼lb snow peas
1 mango, peeled and cut into chunks
1 fresh pineapple, peeled and cut into chunks
Red plums, halved and stoned

MARINADE

½ cup olive oil
1 tbsp curry powder (or to taste)
½ cup fresh lime juice

METHOD

Make sure the vein running along the back of the shrimp is

removed and also any tough muscle attached to the sea scallops. If the plums are large, cut them into quarters. Break off the stems of the snow peas and pull backwards to remove the stringy fibers.

Place the ingredients on the skewers in the following manner: pork with pineapple and plum, alternating the ingredients, shrimp with snow peas, scallops with mango. Use separate skewers for any leftover peas or fruit. Mix the marinade ingredients and brush over the prepared skewers. Grill over hot coals or on a preheated grill for 8-10 minutes, basting frequently. Do not have the racks too close to the coals and remember that the scallops and shrimp will cook a bit faster than the pork. Serve the skewers over rice.

DANIEL ROUTHIER,
DEAN'S MILL FARM,
STONINGTON, CT

BAKED WHOLE BLUEFISH

This is an impressive way to serve this popular New England fish for a dinner party. The colorful garnish dresses it up and gives extra flavor.

Preparation Time: 30 minutes
Cooking Time: 1 hour 15 minutes
Oven Temperature: 250°F
Serves: 4

INGREDIENTS

1 bluefish, 18–20 inches long
2 lemons
¾ cup white wine or vermouth
½ cup olive oil
¼ lb butter
¼ cup water
Ground black pepper
1 large red onion, chopped
Fresh chives, sage, thyme, oregano, dill and parsley
½ cup shrimp (optional)
4 scallops (optional)
1 cup small whole mushrooms
¼ lb whole cherry tomatoes, stems removed

Purée of Squash (top), Grilled Bluefish with Lime-Ginger Marinade (center left), Corn Pudding (center right) and Baked Whole Bluefish (bottom).

GARNISH

Lemon wedges
Parsley sprigs
Dill sprigs
Whole cherry tomatoes

METHOD

Thoroughly grease a large, shallow baking pan with the olive oil and place in the fish, head and tail on. Stuff the belly of the fish with whole fresh herbs and chopped onion. Pour the olive oil over the fish and sprinkle with chopped herbs and a pinch of pepper and salt. Dot with butter and pour over the juice of two lemons, wine and water. Place in a preheated oven and baste occasionally while cooking for 1 hour. Remove the dish from the oven and add the shrimp and scallops, if using. Also add the mushrooms and cherry tomatoes. Replace in the oven and cook for 10-15 minutes more. Allow the fish to stand in the cooking liquid for 15 minutes then remove to a warm platter for serving. Place the shrimp, scallops, tomatoes and mushrooms around the fish with the lemon wedges, sprigs or parsley, dill and additional tomatoes.

ARNOLD COPPER,
DEAN'S MILL FARM,
STONINGTON, CT

CORN PUDDING

Corn has been a valuable food throughout the history of this country. It was the corn crop that saved the Massachusetts Bay Colony and corn recipes found their way to Connecticut from there.

Preparation Time: 20 minutes
Cooking Time: 45 minutes
Oven Temperature: 350°F
Serves: 6-8

INGREDIENTS

2 cups Carnation milk or thin cream
2 cups canned or fresh corn
2 tbsps melted butter
2 tsps sugar
1 tsp salt
¼ tsp pepper
3 eggs, well beaten

METHOD

Add the milk, corn, butter, sugar and seasonings to the eggs. Pour into a well greased casserole and bake in a moderate oven for about 45 minutes or until the pudding is set. Insert a knife into the center of the pudding and if it comes out clean the pudding is done. For variety, add ¼ cup chopped green peppers or pimento, ½ cup minced ham or chopped mushrooms.

ISABELLA WITT,
DEAN'S MILL FARM,
STONINGTON, CT

PURÉE OF SQUASH

A creamy vegetable purée is just the thing to serve with grilled or roast poultry, meat or game. Half and half or cream instead of milk makes it extra rich.

Preparation Time: 20 minutes
Cooking Time: 20-30 minutes
Serves: 4-6

INGREDIENTS

1 large butternut squash, peeled and cubed
1 tart apple, peeled and cubed
½ cup milk, cream or half and half
2 tbsps butter
Freshly ground nutmeg

METHOD

Bring the squash and apple to the boil with just enough water to cover. Drain well and add the butter, milk and nutmeg and mash together well. Add more butter, if desired, and milk to bring to the consistency of mashed potatoes.

DANIEL ROUTHIER,
DEAN'S MILL FARM,
STONINGTON, CT

BEEF BOUILLON

This soup traces its ancestry back to the elegant French consommé. This version calls for the addition of port wine, which makes it very rich. Do not add the mushrooms to the soup too soon or they will overcook. Use this recipe for an impressive first course.

Preparation Time: 30 minutes for home-made
bouillon
15 minutes for canned bouillon
Cooking Time: 1 hour for home-made
15 minutes for canned
Serves: 6

INGREDIENTS

6 cups prepared beef bouillon
1 cup port wine
6 large raw mushrooms, washed, dried and sliced very
thinly

METHOD

Heat the bouillon and port to a simmer, but do not allow to boil. Place several slices of raw mushroom in the bottom of each soup bowl. Fill the bowl at the last minute with the hot bouillon. Sprinkle with some freshly chopped parsley, if desired.

MARGARETHE Z. THOMAS,
DEAN'S MILL FARM,
STONINGTON, CT

NEW ENGLAND POT ROAST

The origin of pot roast is a little difficult to track down, although it has been a popular dish in New England for years and years. The French and German influence, though, is quite clear. This dish was traditionally cooked in an iron pot which became known as a Dutch oven.

Preparation Time: 30 minutes
Cooking Time: 3 hours
Serves: 10

INGREDIENTS

4lbs top or bottom round of beef
4 tbsps butter
1 clove garlic, chopped
1 tsp flour
1 tbsp butter
¾ cup chopped onion
2 cups water

1 cup red wine
1 carrot, sliced
10 peppercorns
3 sprigs parsley
1 bay leaf
2 whole cloves
Pinch allspice
Salt to taste
¼ tsp ground pepper

METHOD

Melt the butter in a Dutch oven and sauté the onion and garlic until brown. Add the meat and brown well on all sides. Add the remaining ingredients, except the remaining butter and the flour. Bring to the boil and simmer for about 3 hours, or until the meat is tender. Add more wine and water as needed. Remove the meat to a heated platter and boil the liquid to reduce it by half. Put the remaining butter in a deep saucepan and stir in the flour. Pour on the reduced cooking liquid and stir well. Allow the sauce to boil until thickened. Strain the sauce and pour some over the meat. Serve the rest of the sauce separately.

MARGARETHE Z. THOMAS,
DEAN'S MILL FARM,
STONINGTON, CT

MIXED SALAD

This salad can serve a dual purpose. Arrange it attractively on individual plates for an elegant but easy first course. Alternatively, toss it all together for an informal meal. Prepare the dressing ahead of time to allow the flavors to blend.

Preparation Time: 15 minutes
Serves: 4-6

INGREDIENTS

SALAD
1 lb spinach, well washed and torn into bite-size pieces
1 small bunch chicory
1 small can mandarine oranges

Overleaf: (clockwise from top center) Baked Acorn Squash, Mixed Salad, New England Pot Roast, Beef Bouillon and Spinach Onion Casserole.

6-8 mushrooms, thinly sliced
1 red onion, thinly sliced

MUSTARD DRESSING

2 cloves garlic
½ tsp dry mustard or 1 tsp prepared mustard
3 drops Tabasco
6 tbsps wine vinegar
12 tbsps olive oil

METHOD

Pat the spinach dry or dry in a salad spinner. Combine with the remaining salad ingredients in a large bowl or on individual plates. Place the dressing ingredients in a blender or food processor and combine until well mixed. Leave to stand and pour over the salad to serve.

DANIEL ROUTHIER,
DEAN'S MILL FARM,
STONINGTON, CT

SPINACH ONION CASSEROLE

This casserole is ideal for a buffet. It must be prepared well in advance, but it is simplicity itself to assemble and can be doubled or tripled in quantity with no problems.

Preparation Time: 15 minutes plus 2-3 hours standing
Cooking Time: 20 minutes
Oven Temperature: 350°F
Serves: 4-5

INGREDIENTS

1¼ lbs fresh or frozen spinach
1½ oz dehydrated onion soup mix
1 pint sour cream
2 tbsps sherry
1 small can French fried onions

METHOD

Cook the spinach and drain thoroughly, pressing out as much water as possible. Combine spinach, onion soup mix, sour cream and sherry and spoon into a casserole dish. Let stand 2-3 hours at room temperature to blend the flavors. Sprinkle

the top with French fried onions and cook about 20 minutes or until bubbling. Serve immediately.

MARGARETHE Z. THOMAS,
DEAN'S MILL FARM,
STONINGTON, CT

BOILED NEW ENGLAND DINNER

This has been a continual favorite in the New England states and across the country. The parsnips are a delicious idea as a substitute for the turnips which traditionally appear. It wasn't until the 1730s that potatoes were included.

Preparation Time: 30 minutes
Cooking Time: 3-3½ hours
Serves: 8

INGREDIENTS

4lbs corned beef brisket
8 medium-sized potatoes
6-8 carrots, peeled
1 head cabbage
6-8 small parsnips, peeled

METHOD

Rinse the corned beef and cook for 3-3½ hours, covered with water. Slice the vegetables, add them to the beef and cook until tender. Season with salt and pepper and serve sprinkled with chopped parsley.

MRS. MARY ROY,
DEAN'S MILL FARM,
STONINGTON, CT

BAKED ACORN SQUASH

Squash was a popular vegetable with the first colonists because it was easy to grow in a harsh climate and it kept very well. Half an acorn squash cooked in its skin makes a very attractive side dish and is especially good with poulty, pork or ham. The dash of rum makes an interesting addition.

Facing page: New England Boiled Dinner.

CONNECTICUT

Preparation Time: 20 minutes
Cooking Time: 1½ hours
Oven Temperature: 325°F
Serves: 8

INGREDIENTS

4 acorn squash, cut in half, seeds removed
8 tbsps butter
8 tbsps brown sugar
8 tbsps dark rum

METHOD

Place the cut acorn squash in a shallow baking dish and add 1 tbsp of butter, brown sugar and dark rum to the center of each squash half. Bake 1½ hours or until the fork pierces the squash easily. Be careful not to poke holes in the outer skin. During the cooking, spoon some of the liquid from the center over the sides of the squash.

MARGARETHE Z. THOMAS,
DEAN'S MILL FARM,
STONINGTON, CT

GRILLED VEGETABLES

Cooking food outdoors has long been popular in the United States; it was in colonial times and still is to the present day. Vegetables are delicious with just a hint of charcoal taste and these can be used to accompany grilled meat or for a vegetarian barbecue.

Preparation Time: 30 minutes
Cooking Time: 15-20 minutes

INGREDIENTS

Any combination of the following: summer squash, zucchini squash, yellow onions, yellow, green or red peppers, scallions, large mushrooms, tomatoes, eggplant or other seasonal fresh vegetables

MARINADE

1 stick butter, melted
½ cup fresh lemon juice
Freshly ground pepper

Right: Grilled Vegetables.

M E T H O D

Prepare the vegetables as follows: cut summer squash and zucchini squash in half, lengthwise. Cut yellow onions in half around the equator and leave the peels on. Cut the peppers in half, lengthwise and remove the seeds but leave on the stems. Trim the root ends and the thin green ends of the scallions. Trim the stems from the mushrooms. Remove the stems from the tomatoes. Cut the eggplant in half, lengthwise or in quarters if very large. Melt the butter in a small saucepan and add the lemon juice and the pepper. Cook the onions, squashes and eggplant first as they will take the longest to cook. Baste the cut side of all the vegetables and place cut side down on the grill. When they have lightly browned, turn and baste well again. Complete the cooking of the squash, onions and eggplant on their skin sides. Halfway through their cooking time, add the peppers, mushrooms, scallions and tomatoes. Baste all the vegetables well as they cook. If using cherry tomatoes, warm them on the grill for a few seconds, but not for long or they will split and become mushy. The marinade is also excellent when used with chicken.

DANIEL ROUTHIER,
DEAN'S MILL FARM,
STONINGTON, CT

GRILLED BLUEFISH WITH LIME-GINGER MARINADE

Here is yet another recipe for this popular fish, but this time in an oriental style. Besides adding flavor to this fish, the marinade helps to keep it moist while grilling.

Preparation Time: 15 minutes plus 3 hours chilling
Cooking Time: 8-10 minutes
Serves: 2

I N G R E D I E N T S

MARINADE
½ cup fresh lime juice
1 tsp grated lime rind
3 cloves garlic, crushed

½ cup olive oil
2 tsps minced fresh ginger
Salt and pepper
2 large bluefish fillets, with skin

M E T H O D

Mix the marinade ingredients together and pour over the bluefish fillets in a shallow dish. Turn to coat both sides well and cover. Marinate for 3 hours in the refrigerator. On hot charcoal or in a preheated gas grill, cook the flesh side of the fillet first for approximately 5 minutes or until the fish is lightly browned. Turn over and baste the fish well with the marinade. Grill the skin side an additional 3 to 5 minutes or until the fish is thoroughly cooked. Reheat the marinade and transfer the fish to a hot serving platter. Pour the remaining marinade over the fish to serve. This marinade is good with other oily fish such as tuna or salmon.

DANIEL ROUTHIER,
DEAN'S MILL FARM,
STONINGTON, CT

FRUIT TART

This dessert is really a combination of pie and fruit crisp. The base is a variation of French pie pastry and the topping bakes crisp and sweet. It is delicious with any seasonal fruit.

Preparation Time: 25-30 minutes
Cooking Time: 30 minutes
Oven Temperature: 350°F
Makes: 1 pie

I N G R E D I E N T S

CRUST
1 cup flour
3 tbsps sugar
¼ tsp baking powder
4 tbsps cold butter
1 egg
6 drops almond extract

FILLING
3 cups fruit such as peaches, blueberries, strawberries
or apples
Lemon juice

Facing page: Fruit Tart.

TOPPING

2 tbsps flour
2 tbsps sugar
3 tbsps butter
Pinch cinnamon

METHOD

Combine the flour, sugar and baking powder in a food processor and process once or twice to sift. Add the butter and cut in until the mixture resembles fine bread crumbs. Add the egg and the almond extract and mix to bring the pastry together. Press into a pie plate evenly over the bottom and sides. Prepare the fruit and sprinkle lemon juice over. Pile the fruit into the pastry and set it aside. Melt the butter for the topping and stir in the remaining ingredients. Sprinkle over the fruit and bake for 30 minutes in a moderate oven, or until the crust is brown and the fruit is tender and bubbling.

DANIEL ROUTHIER,
DEAN'S MILL FARM,
STONINGTON, CT

AUNT HELEN'S CREAM CHEESECAKE

Cheesecake is one of the most popular desserts in the United States. This one makes use of New England's delicious blueberries in a sauce that complements the cake's velvety richness.

Preparation Time: 30 minutes
Cooking Time: 1 hour 10 minutes
Makes: 1 cake

INGREDIENTS

CRUST

2 cups zwieback crumbs
½ cup granulated sugar
½ cup melted, unsalted butter

FILLING

1½lbs softened cream cheese
2 tsps vanilla extract
1 cup granulated sugar
5 eggs

TOPPING

1 quart sour cream
¼ cup granulated sugar
2 tsps vanilla extract

BLUEBERRY SAUCE

1 cup granulated sugar
2 tsps cornstarch
¼ tsp ground nutmeg
Pinch salt
1 cup cold water
2½ cups fresh blueberries, picked over and cleaned,
or 4 cups frozen blueberries
3 tsps lemon juice

METHOD

Combine the crust ingredients together and press into a 10″ spring pan. Press the mixture 2 inches up the sides of the pan and cover the bottom completely. Blend the filling ingredients together using a mixer or food processor, adding the eggs one at a time. Pour into the prepared crust and bake at 325°F for 1 hour. Remove the cake from the oven and let stand for 5 minutes. Mix the topping ingredients together and pour over the cake. Return the cake to the oven, raise the temperature to 375°F and bake for 8 minutes. Remove the cake from the oven and allow to cool on a rack at room temperature. Cover and chill thoroughly in the refrigerator, preferably overnight. Serve cut into 12 to 16 portions. To prepare the blueberry sauce, combine all the ingredients except the blueberries and lemon juice and cook over medium heat in a stainless steel pan. Stir constantly until the mixture thickens and comes to the boil. Cook about 2 minutes or until the mixture clears. Add the blueberries and return to the boil. Remove from the heat and immediately add the lemon juice. Add more lemon juice if necessary to adjust the sweetness. Serve a spoonful of sauce over or around the cheesecake slices.

NOAH'S RESTAURANT OF STONINGTON, CT

GINGERSNAPS

These have always been a favorite in American cookie jars. They were long considered a roll cookie, which meant that the dough was formed into a long sausage shape, chilled until firm and sliced. Now the dough can be shaped into balls or simply dropped on the greased baking sheets. Crushed and mixed with butter and sugar, they make a nice change from the usual graham cracker crust for pies or cheesecake.

Preparation Time: 25 minutes
Cooking Time: 12-15 minutes per batch
Oven Temperature: 250°F
Makes: 3 dozen cookies

INGREDIENTS

2 cups flour
2 tsps baking soda
1 tsp cinnamon
½ tsp salt
½ tsp ginger
¼ tsp ground cloves
¾ cup shortening
1 cup sugar
1 egg, well beaten
¼ cup molasses

METHOD

Sift the dry ingredients together and set them aside. In a separate bowl, beat the shortening until light and gradually add the sugar. Beat in the eggs and molasses and then put in the dry ingredients. Form the dough into 1 inch balls and place them about 2 inches apart on greased cookie sheets. Flatten them with a fork and bake 12-15 minutes or until crisp. Allow to cool on the cookie sheet for 1 minute before transferring to a cooling rack. If the dough is too soft to shape, drop by teaspoonfuls onto the cookie sheets or refrigerate the dough until firm.

MRS. RITA ROUTHIER,
DEAN'S MILL FARM,
STONINGTON, CT

CHOCOLATE CHIP COOKIES

Everyone has a slightly different version of this popular cookie. Long before chocolate was sold in small morsels, cooks had to cut up bars of chocolate into small chips, hence the name. These cookies were also known as Tollhouse Cookies, after the Tollhouse Restaurant, where the owner, Ruth Wakefield made these cookies popular.

Preparation Time: 20 minutes
Cooking Time: 10-12 minutes per batch

Oven Temperature: 375°F
Makes: approximately 3 dozen

INGREDIENTS

1 cup flour
½ tsp baking soda
½ tsp salt
½ cup shortening
½ cup sugar
¼ cup firmly packed brown sugar
1 egg
1 6oz package chocolate bits
1 tsp vanilla
½ cup nut meats

METHOD

Put the flour, baking soda and salt into a bowl. Cream the shortening in a separate bowl and add the sugar gradually, creaming together until light and fluffy. Add the egg and beat in thoroughly. Add the dry ingredients in two parts and mix well. Finally stir in the chocolate bits, nuts and vanilla and mix well. Drop from a teaspoon, about 2 inches apart, onto ungreased baking sheets. Bake 10-12 minutes or until crisp. Allow to cool 1 minute on the baking sheet and remove to a cooling rack.

MRS. RITA ROUTHIER,
DEAN'S MILL FARM,
STONINGTON, CT

BAKED APPLES

Baked apples are a comforting, warming dessert that has long been popular in the United States. Sugar, cinnamon and raisins form the classic filling for baked apples, but the addition of slivered almonds and sherry make this version a bit special.

Preparation Time: 20 minutes
Cooking Time: 30-40 minutes
Oven Temperature: 350°F
Serves: 4

Overleaf: Gingersnaps (top left), Chocolate Chip Cookies (bottom left) and Aunt Helen's Cream Cheesecake (right).

INGREDIENTS

4 large, tart apples
½ cup brown sugar
2 tbsps raisins
1 tsp cinnamon
½ cup slivered almonds
1 cup water
3 tbsps sherry

METHOD

Core the apples, leaving half an inch at the bottom. Mix the filling ingredients together and fill the apples with the mixture. Place them in a shallow baking dish and add the water and sherry. Bake 30-40 minutes, until soft but not mushy. Serve with ice cream and spoon over the cooking liquid.

MARGARETHE Z. THOMAS,
DEAN'S MILL FARM,
STONINGTON, CT

BLUEBERRY MUFFINS

Blueberries grow in abundance in the New England states and all over the country as well. Wild blueberries ripen in July, August and September and are a real treat to look forward to. Serve these light, tender muffins piping hot.

Preparation Time: 20 minutes
Cooking Time: 20 minutes
Oven Temperature: 400°F
Makes: 12 muffins

INGREDIENTS

1½ cups flour
½ cup sugar
¼ tsp salt
2 tsps baking powder
1 egg
¼ cup oil
½ cup milk
1 cup blueberries

METHOD

Mix the flour, sugar, salt and baking powder and set aside. Mix the egg and oil until well blended. Add the wet ingredients to the dry ingredients, stirring in gradually. Fold in the blueberries and pour the batter into greased and floured muffin pans or pans lined with cupcake papers. Half-fill each hole in the pan. Bake for 20 minutes, or until well risen and nicely browned.

MRS. MARY ROY,
DEAN'S MILL FARM,
STONINGTON, CT

CRISP CRUSTY WAFFLES

Waffles date from the beginning of the 19th century in the United States. Early waffle irons were put on top of the stove and even over an open flame, but they had to be turned at least once during cooking. When electric waffle irons were invented, waffles became even more popular. In addition to breakfast, waffles are often served for lunch or for a light supper. You can top them with butter and syrup or honey, creamed chicken or seafood, ham or bacon, or with fruit and ice cream or whipped cream for dessert.

Preparation Time: 20 minutes
Cooking Time: 5 minutes per waffle
Makes: 6-7 waffles

INGREDIENTS

2 cups flour
4 tsps baking powder
1 tsp salt
3 eggs, separated
1¾ cups milk
½ cup salad oil
Pinch sugar

METHOD

Sift together the flour, salt and baking powder. Beat the egg whites until stiff. Beat the yolks until light and add milk and oil. Stir the yolk and flour mixture together and fold in the egg whites. Heat the waffle iron and grease well. Spoon some of the mixture into the waffle iron and lower the lid. Take care not to put in too much batter as it will spread. Bake until the steam has stopped coming from around the edge of the iron

Facing page: Crisp Crusty Waffles and Blueberry Muffins.

and lift the lid to see if the waffle is nicely browned. If not, lower the lid and continue cooking for another minute or two until crisp.

MRS. RITA ROUTHIER,
DEAN'S MILL FARM,
STONINGTON, CT

APPLE CRISP

Apple crisp is an old-fashioned dessert that has remained immensely popular over the years. Perhaps this is because it is so easy to make and so good to eat. The topping mixture can be made ahead of time and stored in the refrigerator to be used whenever the desire for apple crisp strikes.

Preparation Time: 25 minutes
Cooking Time: 45 minutes
Oven Temperature: 350°F
Serves: 4-6

INGREDIENTS

6-8 tart apples
½ cup granulated sugar
¼ tsp ground cloves
½ tsp cinnamon
2 tsps lemon juice

TOPPING

¾ cup flour
6 tbsps butter
½ cup brown sugar

METHOD

Peel and slice the apples. Blend the remaining ingredients and toss with the apples to mix thoroughly. Pour into a buttered 1½ quart casserole. Blend the topping ingredients together into a crumbly consistency and sprinkle over the top of the apples. Bake 45 minutes or until the apples are tender and the top is brown and crisp. Serve with cream or vanilla ice cream.

MARGARETHE Z. THOMAS,
DEAN'S MILL FARM,
STONINGTON, CT

Left: (from left) Baked Apples, Apple Butter, Cider Mill Apple Dessert and Apple Crisp.

PUMPKIN RAISIN-NUT BREAD

Raisins and nuts make a nice addition to this spicy bread. Try serving it and the plain pumpkin bread slightly warm, spread with butter or cream cheese.

Preparation Time: 20 minutes
Cooking Time: 1 hour
Oven Temperature: 350°F
Makes: 2 loaves

INGREDIENTS

1 cup vegetable oil
4 eggs, beaten
⅔ cup water
2 cups canned or fresh pumpkin
3½ cups sifted flour
1½ tsps salt
1 tsp ground cloves
2 tsps baking soda
½ tsp baking powder
1 tsp nutmeg
1 tsp cinnamon
2⅔ cups sugar
1 cup raisins
1 cup chopped pecans

METHOD

Grease and flour the loaf pans and set them aside. Combine the oil, eggs, water and pumpkin. Sift in the dry ingredients and blend until moistened. Stir in the raisins and pecans and divide the mixture between the two pans. Bake 1 hour in a preheated oven, or until a knife inserted into the center of the bread comes out clean.

MRS. RITA ROUTHIER,
DEAN'S MILL FARM,
STONINGTON, CT

JOHNNYCAKES

Indians made their corn bread by grinding corn, mixing it with water and baking it in a cake-like patty over a hot fire. These were known as Journey Cakes because they were easy to prepare when travelling, and somehow came to be called Johnnycakes.

Preparation Time: 10 minutes
Cooking Time: 11 minutes
Makes: 8-10 cakes

INGREDIENTS

1 cup cornmeal
1 tsp salt
1¼ cups water
1 tsp sugar

METHOD

Mix the cornmeal and salt and sugar together. Boil the water and beat in gradually until the batter is smooth, but very thick (it may not be necessary to add all the water). Drop onto a well greased, hot griddle and fry over medium heat for 6 minutes. Turn over and cook on the other side for 5 minutes. Serve immediately.

TRADITIONAL RECIPE

PUMPKIN BREAD

The addition of pumpkin in this quick bread recipe makes for a very moist bread with a beautiful color.

Preparation Time: 20 minutes
Cooking Time: 1 hour
Oven Temperature: 350°F
Makes: 1 9" x 5" loaf

INGREDIENTS

1 cup canned pumpkin
2 eggs
2 cups flour
¾ cup sugar
¼ tsp cinnamon
¼ tsp nutmeg
⅛ tsp ground cloves
1 tsp baking soda

Facing page: Pumpkin Bread (top left), Pumpkin Raisin-Nut Bread (top right), Johnnycakes (bottom left) and Indian Pudding (bottom right).

METHOD

Mix the pumpkin and the eggs together well and sift in the dry ingredients. Fold together and put into a well greased loaf pan. Bake 1 hour until a knife inserted into the center of the bread comes out clean.

ANNETTE MINER
CIDER MILL
STONINGTON, CT

CIDER MILL APPLE DESSERT

This is a type of apple crisp and is a delicious way to use very tart apples. The topping contains 1 whole cup of brown sugar which cooks to a caramel crispness.

Preparation Time: 25 minutes
Cooking Time: 30 minutes
Oven Temperature: 350°F
Makes: 1 9″ dessert

INGREDIENTS

4 cups sliced apples
½ cup water
1 cup flour
1 cup light brown sugar
1 tsp cinnamon
½ cup butter, cut into small pieces

METHOD

Peel the apples and slice them thinly into a 9-inch-round pie dish. Pour over the water and then mix the remaining ingredients until the pieces are the size of small peas. Spread the topping over the apples and bake until the apples are tender and the crust is brown and crisp, about 30 minutes.

ANNETTE MINER
CIDER MILL
STONINGTON, CT

WASSAIL BOWL

This punch was the symbol of Christmas hospitality in the colonies, and traces its ancestry back to England. It can easily be made days in advance and kept in a cool place.

Preparation Time: 15 minutes
Cooking Time: 15 minutes
Makes: 1 gallon

INGREDIENTS

1 gallon cider
1 tbsp whole allspice
8oz brown sugar
1 tbsp whole cloves
2 whole cinnamon sticks
2 blades mace
¼ tsp salt
2 lemons, thinly sliced
2 oranges, thinly sliced
2 cups dark rum

METHOD

Heat the cider in a large pot and add the brown sugar. Put the allspice, cinnamon sticks, cloves and mace in a square of cheesecloth and tie to make a small bag. Add to the cider and bring it to the boil. Allow to simmer for 15 minutes. Remove the bag of spices and add the rum and fruit slices just before serving. Serve hot.

DANIEL ROUTHIER,
DEAN'S MILL FARM,
STONINGTON, CT

INDIAN PUDDING

The preparation of this pudding cannot be hurried. Cornmeal must thicken slowly and absorb the milk gradually or it will be hard and granular and the pudding will be spoiled. The traditional Indian version was, of course, much simpler, but the addition of apples, raisins and nuts makes this pudding fit for company.

Preparation Time: 25 minutes
Cooking Time: 55 minutes
Oven Temperature: 350°F
Serves: 8

INGREDIENTS

5 cups milk
½ cup cornmeal
1 cup dark molasses

¼ *cup butter*
1 tsp salt
2 eggs, well beaten
1 cup apples, cored and diced
½ *cup raisins*
½ *cup chopped walnuts*
½ *tsp cinnamon*

M E T H O D

Bring the milk to the boil and slowly add the cornmeal, stirring constantly. Cook over very gentle heat or in the top part of a double boiler for about 25 minutes or until the cornmeal thickens. Add the molasses and the remaining ingredients. Pour into a well greased round baking dish. Bake for about 30 minutes. Serve warm with whipped cream or vanilla ice cream.

MRS. LINDA ROUTHIER,
DEAN'S MILL FARM,
STONINGTON, CT

APPLE BUTTER

Making a thick spread from very ripe fruit such as apples, plums or peaches is an old Colonial culinary art. If no sugar or honey was available, the fruit furnished the sweetness all on its own. Butters were often cooked over open fires in the back yard in large copper kettles and constantly stirred with long wooden paddles.

Preparation Time: 1 hour

Cooking Time: 2-3 hours
Makes: Approximately 6 pints

I N G R E D I E N T S

10lbs tart red apples (approximately ½ bushel)
1 tsp whole allspice
1 tsp whole cloves
2-3 sticks cinnamon
2 sliced lemons or limes
2 quarts apple cider
2 cups granulated sugar

M E T H O D

Wash, core and slice the apples but do not peel them. Place in a large, deep, heavy-based pan with the spices and lemons or limes. Add boiling water to almost cover, and cook slowly, uncovered, until the apples are slushy in consistency. This takes approximately 1 hour. If the cinnamon sticks have not softened, remove them from the mixture and purée in a food processor or food mill. Rinse out the pot and add the apple cider. Bring to the boil and stir in the sugar. After the sugar dissolves, add the apple purée and reduce the heat. Cook over very low heat, stirring occasionally, but do not scrape the bottom. Continue cooking slowly until the apple butter is ready to spread. To test it, spread a tablespoon of the mixture on a piece of frozen bread. If it sets immediately, the apple butter is done. Pour the hot apple butter into sterilized jars, seal and store.

PAUL MULLINS,
DEAN'S MILL FARM,
STONINGTON, CT

RHODE ISLAND

Rhode Island contains two major islands within its boundaries – Rhode, which gives its name to the whole state, and Block. For all its small size – it is the smallest state in the Union – it has had a complicated and fiercely independent history. The four earliest towns – Providence, Portsmouth, Newport, and Warwick – were all settled by different groups. For nearly 17 years after the first settlement was founded the settlers could not agree on a common form of government.

Colonial Rhode Island was the very cradle of liberty; in fact, one of the first acts of rebellion against the British Crown occurred here in the period leading up to the American Revolution. The Sugar Act, passed by Parliament in 1764, cut into the profitable rum trade, and the Rhode Islanders burned and sank a British customs ship in retaliation for enactment of a law they thought unfair.

RHODE ISLAND

The state has a beautiful coastline of sandy beaches, sheltered coves, and harbors, so it comes as no surprise that fish and seafood have always been a favorite with Rhode Islanders. Two of the principal New England fish – butterfish and bluefish – are abundant in the state's coastal waters. Butterfish, sometimes called dollarfish, are small, delicate creatures that are excellent fried or cooked in butter on a griddle. Baby butterfish, no longer than a little finger, are usually deep-fried until very crisp, then eaten whole. Bluefish have a reputation as the gluttons of the sea, sometimes eating twice their weight per day of smaller fish. When large, bluefish tend to be oily, and while not recommended for frying, they are delicious baked or broiled. When they are small, however, they are known as snapper blues, and are delicious pan-fried. Bluefish are also found in the Mediterranean, so it makes perfect sense to include them in a North American version of Bouillabaisse. And that is just what French immigrants did when they settled in Rhode Island!

A sizeable Italian community in Providence shows its influence in many recipes, including Steamed Mussels, with tomatoes, basil, garlic and olive oil; and Stuffed Quahogs, with colorful red and green peppers and a grated cheese topping. But New England's favorite soup, clam chowder, is also enjoyed here. Barbecues, surely the most relaxed style of cooking and eating, are extremely popular. Lamb is sometimes roasted in the traditional way, on a spit in a reflector oven, until it is "done to a turn."

The formal side of Rhode Island has been in existence since the mid-18th century, when the famous yachting center at Newport developed. The area became a symbol of wealth and elegance in the 19th century and it was in this extravagant age that most of the mansions, amusingly called cottages, were built.

One such house is Hammersmith Farm which, with its gracious rooms and magnificent setting, was a summer White House for President and Mrs. Kennedy and their children. As you would expect from its elegant surroundings, the recipes are elegant, too, having been influenced by classic French cuisine. For instance, Chateaubriand is a well-known French method of serving beef tenderloin. Though they are not a typical French garnish, Rhode Islanders often serve delightful stuffed baked potatoes as a side dish. The Grand Marnier Cake is based on a famous French gateau, but is given the whimsical touch of chocolate liqueur-filled cups on top. French purists may feel outraged, but then, that is just the independent spirit of Rhode Island at work again!

Facing page: Strawberry Cheesecake

WATCH HILL BOUILLABAISSE

Give this famous dish from Southern France some American style by using the fish native to Rhode Island. Choose from bluefish, weakfish or sea trout, sea bass, black bass, flounder, swordfish steaks, squid, oysters or quahogs. Serve it with a native wine as well, such as Sakonnet 'Eye of the Storm' from Little Compton, Rhode Island.

Preparation Time: 25 minutes
Cooking Time: 15-20 minutes
Serves: 2 as a main course or 4 as an appetizer

INGREDIENTS

1lb fresh lobster, split lengthwise and disjointed
4 small hard-shell clams (littlenecks or cherry stones)
4 soft-shell clams (steamers)
3-4oz fresh sea scallops
½ cup clear fish stock (clam juice can be substituted)
4oz peeled Italian tomatoes, coarsely chopped
12 pieces firm-meated fish
2 tbsps olive oil
½ cup dry white wine
1 tsp chopped shallots
½ tbsp chopped parsley
Pinch saffron
3 crushed black peppercorns

METHOD

Sauté the shallots in olive oil without allowing them to color. Add the parsley, saffron, peppercorns and wine. Bring to the boil and allow to reduce slightly. Add the tomatoes, fish stock, fish and shellfish. Cover tightly and simmer gently until the clams open. Arrange the fish and shellfish in large soup plates and spoon over the liquid. Serve immediately.

THE OLYMPIA TEA ROOM,
BAY STREET, WATCH HILL, RI

BUTTER FISH

These are light, tasty fish caught in waters of New England. Leave on the head and tail and serve them on the griddle on

Right: enough to delight any chef – a tempting array of fresh Rhode Island seafood.

which they are cooked. They are delicious for breakfast with scrambled eggs.

Preparation Time: 20 minutes
Cooking Time: 3 minutes
Serves: 4

INGREDIENTS

4-8 butter fish, gutted
2-4 tbsps butter
Lemon slices

METHOD

Place 1-2 fish per person on a hot griddle with butter and cook over a low heat for about 3 minutes. The fish may not need to be turned. Garnish each fish with half a thin slice of lemon. Serve as a side dish at any meal.

STEVEN P. MACK, CHASE HILL FARM,
ASHAWAY, RI

CHATEAUBRIAND (ROAST TENDERLOIN MADEIRA)

Hammersmith Farm has a long history. It was established in 1640 and throughout the years has been owned by just three families. Like the house and grounds where Jacqueline Bouvier had the reception after her wedding to John F. Kennedy, the recipe for Chateaubriand is truly elegant.

Preparation Time: 40 minutes
Cooking Time: 1 hour
Serves: 6

INGREDIENTS

2-3lbs beef tenderloin in 1 piece
Butter

MADEIRA SAUCE

1 cup beef consommé mixed with 2 tsps cornstarch
¼ cup dry Madeira
¼ cup butter

Facing page: Butter Fish.
Overleaf: Chateaubriand (Roast Tenderloin Madeira) (top center) and Poached Salmon with Dill Sauce (bottom left).

GARNISHES

Baked stuffed potatoes with Parmesan cheese
Small Belgian carrots
Baby onions
Asparagus
Artichoke hearts

TOMATO TIMBALES WITH BROCCOLI

6 tomatoes
6oz broccoli flowerets
Parmesan cheese
3 tbsps butter

METHOD

Fold under the thin end of the meat and tie the tenderloin at intervals with thin string. Spread the meat with butter and roast on a rack in a roasting pan for 25 minutes in a moderate oven. Cook the carrots and onions in water for about 10 minutes. Add the asparagus and artichoke hearts after 5 minutes. Drain all the vegetables and sauté them in garlic butter to finish cooking. To prepare the timbales, blanch the broccoli flowerets in boiling salted water for 2 minutes. Cut off the rounded ends of the tomatoes and scoop out the pulp and seeds. Stuff with the blanched broccoli, sprinkle with Parmesan cheese and dot with butter. Bake in a moderate oven for 10 minutes. Prepare the baked stuffed potatoes in advance and finish cooking with the tomato and broccoli timbales. When the meat and garnishes are cooked, heat the consommé and the cornstarch in a small saucepan, stirring constantly until the mixture comes to the boil. Add the Madeira and cook until slightly thickened. Swirl in the butter and serve the sauce with the Chateaubriand.

PETER T. CROWLEY
LA FORGE CASINO RESTAURANT,
NEWPORT

POACHED SALMON WITH DILL SAUCE

A whole poached fish is a stunning start to a meal. While looking very impressive, this salmon is easy to prepare and can be cooked ahead of time. The sauce finishes off the appetizer deliciously. A larger salmon makes a main dinner course on a warm summer evening.

Preparation Time: 25 minutes
Cooking Time: 15 minutes

Serves: 6-8

INGREDIENTS

COURT BOUILLON

2 pints water
3½oz dry white wine
½ onion, diced
2 sticks celery, diced
1 carrot, diced
1 tbsp salt
½ tsp pepper
3 whole cloves
1 bay leaf
½ lemon, sliced
3 parsley sprigs
2-3lb whole salmon, cleaned

DILL SAUCE

4 cups sour cream
3 tbsps chopped fresh dill
Juice of 1 small lemon
Pinch salt
Pinch white pepper
1 tsp horseradish

METHOD

Combine the court bouillon ingredients in a large saucepan and bring to the boil. Lower the heat and simmer for 30-45 minutes, strain and allow to cool completely. Place the salmon in a large roasting pan or a fish kettle and pour over the cool court bouillon. Cover and simmer for 15 minutes or place in a preheated 375°F oven for 15 minutes. When the dorsal fin on the back pulls out easily, the fish is cooked. Do not over-cook as the fish will continue to cook slightly as it cools. Lift the fish out of the pan and peel off the skin while still warm. Carefully transfer to a large serving plate and allow to cool. Combine all the sauce ingredients and serve with the salmon. Decorate the plate with watercress if desired.

PETER T. CROWLEY
LA FORGE CASINO RESTAURANT,
NEWPORT

Facing page: Rhode Island Clam Chowder.

RHODE ISLAND CLAM CHOWDER

Clam chowder is one of the earliest and most famous of the seafood stews from the North East. Potatoes found their way into clam chowder in the 18th century, but salt pork and onions were ingredients from the beginning.

Preparation Time: 20 minutes
Cooking Time: 5-6 minutes
Serves: 6-8

INGREDIENTS

3 large New England potatoes, diced and parboiled
1 medium Spanish onion, chopped
12 quahogs
4 crushed black peppercorns
1 tsp fresh thyme
1 bay leaf
1 tsp fresh rosemary, chopped
1 tbsp fresh parsley, chopped
3 pints water
3oz butter or soaked salt pork

METHOD

Cook the potatoes and if using salt pork, place it in a sauté pan over low heat to render the fat. Sauté the chopped onions in the pork fat or butter until soft. Meanwhile, steam the quahogs in water until they open. Save the juice and allow the clams to cool before chopping them. Add the herbs, spices, reserved clam juice, chopped clams and cooked potatoes to the onions and cook until the potatoes are soft and all the flavors are blended.

THE OLYMPIA TEA ROOM,
BAY STREET, WATCH HILL, RI

LEG OF LAMB ROASTED IN A REFLECTOR OVEN

Lamb is an ideal meat to cook by this method because its natural fat keeps the meat moist. The meat is at its best when it is slightly pink in the center. Rosemary complements the flavor of lamb well, but try thyme or mint for a taste variation.

Preparation Time: 15 minutes

RHODE ISLAND

Cooking Time: 1-1½ hours
Serves: 6-8

INGREDIENTS

5-6lb leg of lamb
4 cloves garlic, halved or quartered depending upon size
Fresh or dried rosemary, crushed

METHOD

Push a sharp knife into the meat at 5 inch intervals and insert slivers of garlic into the cuts. Rub with rosemary. Pierce the leg with a skewer and place it in the oven. Cook in front of a slow fire at a distance of approximately 18 inches. Turn every 15 minutes while basting in its own juices. When the meat looks done, cut a small, deep slice to check the color.

STEVEN P. MACK, CHASE HILL FARM,
ASHAWAY, RI

STEAMED MUSSELS

Inexpensive and quick to cook, mussels make an excellent first course. With olive oil, basil and Italian tomatoes in the ingredients, this seafood recipe shows the Italian influence that is so strong in parts of Rhode Island.

Preparation Time: 25 minutes
Cooking Time: 5 minutes
Serves: 2

INGREDIENTS

24 medium mussels, washed and debearded
1 rounded tsp chopped garlic
2 tbsps olive oil
Rosemary, oregano and basil to taste
3oz dry white wine
3 chopped Italian tomatoes

METHOD

Cook the garlic in the olive oil without browning. Add the herbs and white wine and boil well to reduce slightly. Add

Left: Leg of Lamb Roasted in a Reflector Oven. Overleaf: Steamed Mussels (center) and Stuffed Quahogs (bottom).

the tomatoes and mussels, cover and steam until the mussels open (about 5 minutes). Discard any musssels that do not open. Serve with chunks of toasted French bread.

THE OLYMPIA TEA ROOM,
BAY STREET, WATCH HILL, RI

BAKED SEA TROUT IN PARCHMENT

Wrapping delicate food such as fish in paper parcels is an ingenious way of ensuring that all the flavors remain sealed in. For full effect, open the parcels at the table.

Preparation Time: 25 minutes
Cooking Time: 20 minutes
Oven Temperature: 350°F
Serves: 2

INGREDIENTS

1-1¼ lb sea trout fillet (any firm-fleshed fish will do)
4 cleaned mussels
4 Spanish onion slices
4 fresh tomato slices
4 green pepper rings
4 sprigs fresh thyme
4 sprigs fresh sage
2 crushed white peppercorns
Melted butter
White wine

METHOD

Divide the fish into two equal portions and place skinned side down on parchment paper (foil will suffice, but it is not as attractive). Garnish the fish with onion slices, tomato slices and then pepper rings. Place the mussels on top and then the herbs and pepper. Drizzle a little melted butter and wine on the fish and then seal the paper parcels, twisting the ends well. Coat the outsides with additional melted butter and bake for about 20 minutes.

THE OLYMPIA TEA ROOM,
BAY STREET, WATCH HILL, RI

Facing page: Baked Sea Trout in Parchment.

STUFFED QUAHOGS

Quahogs are hard-shell clams that are used for chowder when large, and eaten on the half shell when smaller. To facilitate opening, place well-scrubbed clams in a pan in a moderate oven and heat until they open. Use a strong knife to pry off the top shells. One or two stuffed clams make an excellent hors d'oeuvre or appetizer, more make a great snack or meal. One clam stuffs one shell.

Preparation Time: 20 minutes
Cooking Time: 15 minutes
Oven Temperature: 375°F
Serves: 4

INGREDIENTS

8 quahogs, shelled, poached 3 minutes and chopped
1 onion, chopped
¼ tsp oregano
1 green and 1 red pepper, chopped
1 clove garlic, crushed
3 tbsps butter
Fresh bread crumbs
Grated Romano or Parmesan cheese

METHOD

Sautée the onions and peppers in butter until glassy, add the chopped garlic and cook another 1-2 minutes over low heat. Stir in the chopped clams and an equal amount of fresh bread crumbs. Add about ½ tsp grated cheese per clam. Moisten with additional melted butter and/or clam juice. Stuff into each clam shell half and bake until hot and slightly browned. Serve accompanied with lemon wedges and hot pepper sauce (Tabasco).

THE OLYMPIA TEA ROOM,
BAY STREET, WATCH HILL, RI

STEAMED BLACK BASS ORIENTAL STYLE

Black bass abounds in the Eastern states and it is a popular fish on Rhode Island tables. For an excellent variation on the Oriental theme, the bass may be dredged in rice flour and fried in very hot peanut oil in a wok.

Preparation Time: 25 minutes

Cooking Time: 7-10 minutes
Serves: 2

INGREDIENTS

2 black bass or small sea bass, cleaned and scaled

SAUCE

¾ cup finely chopped green, red and yellow peppers
2 Szechuan peppers
1 tsp chopped garlic
1 tsp chopped fresh ginger
1 tsp fermented black beans
2 tbsps peanut oil
¼ cup dry white wine

METHOD

Steam the whole fish in a Chinese steamer, or improvise with a pan on a rack above boiling water, until the fish flakes easily, about 7-10 minutes. Put the peanut oil in a wok until very hot and fry the peppers until crispy. Add the remaining ingredients and cook to reduce the wine slightly. To serve, ladle over the hot fish on a serving platter.

THE OLYMPIA TEA ROOM,
BAY STREET, WATCH HILL, RI

STRAWBERRY CHEESECAKE

A cheesecake is a dessert that never fails to please. This recipe serves a large gathering, but can easily be cut in half. Strawberries are a favorite choice for topping and they complement the velvety texture so well. For shine, melt a little seedless raspberry jam and brush over the berries, if desired.

Preparation Time: 30 minutes
Cooking Time: 40 minutes
Oven Temperature: 375°F
Makes: 2-10 inch cakes

INGREDIENTS

3lbs cream cheese or curd cheese
15 eggs

Right: Steamed Black Bass Oriental Style.

½ cup sour cream
1 tbsp vanilla extract

GRAHAM CRACKER CRUST

4 cups graham cracker crumbs
1⅓ cups sugar
½lb butter, melted

TOPPING

1lb even-sized strawberries, hulled

METHOD

Soften the cream cheese and gradually beat in the eggs. Stir in the sour cream and vanilla extract. Combine the crust ingredients in a food processor or bowl and mix thoroughly. Press into spring-form pans and pour in the filling. Cook in a moderate oven for 40 minutes. Allow to cool completely before removing from the pans. Decorate the top of each cake with strawberries and brush over jam, if desired.

PETER T. CROWLEY
LA FORGE CASINO RESTAURANT,
NEWPORT

STEAK OVER OPEN FIRE

Chuck steak is a much ignored and inexpensive cut that is delicious when cooked in this manner. Remove the steak just before it is done as it will cook slightly after being taken off the heat. An overcooked steak is no steak at all! Joseph Mack of Chase Hill Farm is the true master of this dish.

Preparation Time: 15 minutes
Cooking Time: 10-20 minutes
Serves: 4

INGREDIENTS

4 6-8oz chuck steaks, cut 1 inch thick
12-16 large mushroom caps
2 large onions, thickly sliced
Sea salt, coarsely ground

METHOD

Rub the sea salt on both sides of the meat and place on a skillet with the mushroom caps and onions. Place the skillet over

Facing page: Steak Over Open Fire. Overleaf: (clockwise from top center) Strawberry Cheesecake, Baked Apples, Dipped Strawberries and Grand Marnier Cake.

a medium fire. The steaks should take only 10-20 minutes to cook, so make sure to cook them last. Turn the steaks only once while cooking and serve with the mushrooms and onions.

STEVEN P. MACK, CHASE HILL FARM,
ASHAWAY, RI

DIPPED STRAWBERRIES

Strawberries dipped in chocolate are a delightful accompaniment to summer desserts or a perfect end to a meal, along with coffee and liqueurs. They can be prepared in advance and kept in the refrigerator until ready to serve, an advantage when entertaining.

Preparation Time: 20-25 minutes, depending on quantity
Cooking Time: 5 minutes

INGREDIENTS

3-4 even-sized strawberries per person, washed and leaves left on
1oz semi-sweet and dark chocolate per serving
1-2 tbsps hot, strong coffee

METHOD

Melt the two chocolates in a double boiler and thin slightly with the hot coffee. Allow to cool slightly. Make sure that the strawberries are dry and dip the pointed end of each one into the chocolate mixture, coating the strawberries about half-way. Allow the chocolate to set completely before serving.

PETER T. CROWLEY
LA FORGE CASINO RESTAURANT,
NEWPORT

BAKED APPLES

Baked apples are one of New England's and America's most popular desserts. Blueberries, with their sweet taste and deep blue-black color, are a particularly good and unusual filling for cored apples. A splash of ginger ale during cooking complements the fresh taste of the apples.

Preparation Time: 15 minutes
Cooking Time: 20-25 minutes

Oven Temperature: 350°F
Serves: 4

INGREDIENTS

4 medium to medium-large apples, cored (Cortland or
MacIntosh apples are a good choice)
1½ cups blueberries, washed
Sugar and cinnamon to taste
1½ cups ginger ale

METHOD

Place the cored apples in a shallow dish and fill with the blueberries. Sprinkle generously with cinnamon and sugar and pour around the ginger ale. Bake in a moderate oven until the apples are tender.

PETER T. CROWLEY
LA FORGE CASINO RESTAURANT,
NEWPORT

AVONDALE SWANS

Use a simple-to-make pastry to make a delightfully imaginative dessert. Fruit purées, chocolate or fudge sauces go well with these ice cream-filled swans. In the Olympia Tea Room, the swans are served swimming in a pool of espresso-flavored chocolate sauce.

Preparation Time: 30 minutes
Cooking Time: 20-30 minutes
Oven Temperature: 400°F
Makes: 3-4 swans

INGREDIENTS

PÂTE A CHOUX

½ cup boiling water
¼ cup butter, cut in small pieces
½ cup all-purpose flour, sifted
2 eggs (at room temperature

FILLING

Ice cream
Whipped cream

Right: Avondale Swans.

METHOD

To prepare the pastry, add the butter to boiling water and stir to melt completely. Blend in the flour and stir to make a stiff dough. Allow to cool slightly and beat in 1 egg at a time until thoroughly blended. Beat until the mixture is smooth and satiny and of thick dropping consistency. It may not be necessary to use all the egg.

To shape the swans, use a small ice cream scoop or spoon to place rounded mounds of the mixture on a baking sheet. Use ¾ of the mixture to shape the bodies of the swans. The swans will take 20-30 minutes to bake, depending on size. Shape the necks and heads by placing the remaining pastry in a pastry bag with a straight, narrow tip. Squeeze out the pastry making a backwards S with a rounded beginning. Bake these separately as they will take less time than the bodies.

To assemble the swans, allow the pastry to cool and cut off the top ⅓ of each body. Split this piece in half; these halves become the wings. Scoop out any soft pastry from the inside of the shells and fill with ice cream. Cover the ice cream with whipped cream, insert the wings and neck into the ice cream and serve the swans swimming in a pool of your favorite sauce.

THE OLYMPIA TEA ROOM,
BAY STREET, WATCH HILL, RI

GRAND MARNIER CAKE

Preparation Time: 1 hour
Cooking Time: 20-30 minutes
Oven Temperature: 375°F
Serves: 8

INGREDIENTS

CAKE
2¼ cups sugar
12 eggs, separated
2¼ cups unsalted butter, melted
¾ cup all-purpose flour sifted with a pinch of salt
Pinch cream of tartar
6oz German sweet chocolate

Facing page: Grand Marnier Cake.

CHOCOLATE CUPS
2oz semi-sweet baking chocolate
1 tsp shortening
Grand Marnier

ICING
2lbs unsalted butter
1 cup shortening
1 cup milk
2 cups powdered sugar, sifted
1 tsp vanilla
2oz dark chocolate, melted

METHOD

First grease and flour 3 8-inch round cake pans. Beat the sugar and egg yolks together until thick and lemon colored. Fold in the melted butter and sift in the flour, salt and cream of tartar. Fold together to mix thoroughly. Beat the egg whites until stiff but not dry. Fold into the cake mixture carefully. Do not over fold. Divide the mixture in thirds and fill 2 of the prepared cake pans with ⅔ of the mixture. Fold the melted chocolate into the remaining third and spoon into the remaining pan. Bake in a moderate oven until the mixture shrinks slightly from the sides of the pans and the tops spring back when touched lightly.

Meanwhile, prepare the chocolate cups. Chop the chocolate into small pieces and combine with the shortening in the top of a double boiler. Melt over gently simmering water, stirring occasionally. When the chocolate is melted, use a pastry brush to paint an even layer of chocolate in each of 8 paper candy cups. Allow to harden, chilling in the refrigerator if necessary.

While the cakes are cooling, prepare the icing. Beat the butter and shortening until light and fluffy. Sift in the powdered sugar and beat until creamy, adding the milk gradually. It may not be necessary to add all the milk. Melt the chocolate and allow it to cool slightly before adding it to ⅓ of the icing. Add vanilla to the remaining ⅔ of the icing.

To assemble the cake, cut the 3 layers in half, horizontally. Sandwich the layers together, alternating the chocolate and vanilla icings, saving enough vanilla icing for the top and sides of the cake. Peel the paper cups carefully away from the chocolate and fill each chocolate cup with Grand Marnier. Place the cups on top of the cake and decorate as shown.

PETER T. CROWLEY
LA FORGE CASINO RESTAURANT,
NEWPORT

MASSACHUSETTS

We learn as schoolchildren that our history began in Massachusetts with the landing of the Pilgrims in 1620. During their first winter, when so many died from an epidemic that also killed vast numbers of native Indians, the Pilgrims learned their first lesson in survival. Both peoples banded together to plant and reap the first harvest, establishing in the process the feast of Thanksgiving as an important and truly American holiday.

All the dishes associated with that feast have become much-loved favorites of generations of Americans. Thanksgiving is still the time when families and friends gather together to celebrate, and kitchens everywhere are filled with busy preparations and the tantalizing aroma of turkey with traditional stuffing and spicy pumpkin pie. Sometimes the pie is made with squash instead of pumpkin, but it is still a delight served with whipped cream. Mashed potatoes, which the English colonists would have known as "creamed" potatoes, are a must with turkey gravy, while candied sweet potatoes often appear alongside. Creamed onions – tiny pearl onions in a rich bechamel sauce – have long been a favorite on the menu. Cranberries are said to be an aid to digestion – which, considering the richness of the food, is just as well! They also provide a splash of color, and their fresh taste combines perfectly with succulent meat.

Cranberries, which grow in peat soil with a layer of sand on top, are true North American berries and are strongly associated with Massachusetts. It wasn't until nearly 200 years after the Pilgrims first ate them that growers began to cultivate them. Though the berries were originally harvested by hand, the invention of a special wooden scoop with fork-like fingers made the work easier. After 1945, mechanical pickers were introduced to speed up the harvest.

The curved peninsula of Cape Cod was a landmark for early explorers. One of these early explorers was so impressed by the many schools of codfish off the cape that he christened it with that name in 1602. Today, the Cape offers ideal vacation spots.

If the Cape is associated with any one food it is seafood. The Pilgrims, anxious for fresh food after the ship's diet of hardtack (hard biscuits), dried fish, cheese, and beer, found the fresh clams, oysters, and mussels very welcome. They began to stew the shellfish and, like the French explorers, found these chowders much to their liking. New England clam chowder is a thick, creamy soup, usually made with potatoes and cubes of salt pork – and lots of clams (but definitely no tomatoes!). New Englanders have very strong opinions about the addition of this ingredient!

The Shakers have had a considerable influence on Massachusetts cooking. A religious sect dedicated to productive labor and a life of perfection, they believed in austerity of decoration and truth to materials, whether wood for furniture or food for the family. So Shaker cuisine is characterized by simple dishes made with easily obtained ingredients for homey, country-style recipes such as Shaker-style Chicken Breasts with a Cider Sauce.

Country-style food is also popular in the Berkshire Hills. Many old villages boast inns and former coach houses where old-fashioned recipes, such as chicken pot pie and split pea soup with ham can be found on the menu.

A local saying boasts that one can get a better meal by accident in Boston than on purpose in most other places. It may be a chauvinistic attitude, but it does stem from a sincere pride. With all the marvelous things to eat in Massachusetts, that pride can be shared by the whole state.

Facing page: The Raw Bar at the Union Oyster House, Boston.

When the pilgrims held a feast to celebrate surviving their first year in the New World, they began a long tradition of family celebrations. Some of the following recipes are traditional, some are variations on the traditional theme and some are contemporary ideas, but all of them can be used to build a memorable Thanksgiving dinner.

BUTTERNUT SQUASH WITH APPLE SOUP

A delicious first course for Thanksgiving dinners.

Preparation Time: 25 minutes
Cooking Time: 20 minutes
Serves: 8

INGREDIENTS

2 carrots, cut in medium-sized dice
2 celery stalks, cut in medium-sized dice
6 Granny Smith apples, peeled,
cored and roughly chopped
2 potatoes, peeled and thinly sliced
1 large butternut squash, peeled,
seeded and roughly chopped
2 tbsps melted butter
1 tsp cinnamon
½ tsp nutmeg
1 quart light cream

GARNISH

Sliced apple

METHOD

Combine the vegetables and butter in a soup pot and stir to coat. Cover the pot and cook over low heat to allow the vegetables to sweat for 10 minutes. Stir in the spices and continue to cook slowly for another 10 minutes. Cook until the vegetables are all very soft. Remove from the heat and purée the vegetables and apples. Heat the cream and add to the soup. Adjust the seasoning and serve hot, garnished with diced apple if desired.

GREEN PEAS WITH MINT

Mint and peas are a naturally good combination.

Preparation Time: 25 minutes
Cooking Time: 15-20 minutes
Serves: 8

INGREDIENTS

1½ lbs shelled fresh peas
1 quart simmering water (not boiling)
Pinch sugar
¼ cup butter
1 bunch fresh mint

METHOD

Drop the peas into the hot water and bring to the simmering point. Cook until tender, 15 to 20 minutes. Place the butter in a sauté pan and add the peas and sugar. Cook to heat through. Chop the mint, reserving 1 sprig for garnish, and add to the peas. Place the reserved mint on top to serve.

SAUSAGE STUFFING FOR ROAST TURKEY

As with all stuffings, this one must not be put into the cavity of the bird until ready to roast.

Preparation Time: 20 minutes
Cooking Time: 15 minutes
Makes: Enough stuffing for 1 large turkey

INGREDIENTS

3 stalks celery, diced
2 onions, diced
5 strips bacon, diced
¼ cup olive oil
6 breakfast sausage links with casings removed
1 tsp oregano
½ tsp basil
¼ tsp thyme
6 cups dry bread crumbs
1 cup chicken stock
¼ cup white wine

METHOD

Combine the celery, onions, bacon and olive oil in a sauté pan. Cook until the vegetables are transparent. Add the sausages and cook them completely. Drain any fat from the pan and add the herbs, breadcrumbs, stock and wine. Stir well and, if dry, add more stock. Stuff the turkey and close the opening. Roast immediately.

CREAMED ONIONS

These are a Thanksgiving classic.

Preparation Time: 25 minutes
Cooking Time: 15-20 minutes
Serves: 8

INGREDIENTS

2lbs pearl onions, peeled
4 quarts boiling salted water
4 tbsps butter
4 tbsps flour
1 quart hot milk
Pinch salt
Pinch nutmeg
Pinch white pepper
Chopped parsley

METHOD

Place the onions and water in a large pot and cook about 10 minutes, or until just barely tender. Drain and set aside. In a saucepan, melt the butter and when foaming add the flour. Gradually beat in the milk and cook over low heat for 8-10 minutes, or until thickened. Add salt, nutmeg and white pepper. Pour the sauce over the onions and heat through before serving. Garnish with the chopped parsley.

CREAMED POTATOES

Creamed is the English term for mashed potatoes.

Preparation Time: 15 minutes
Cooking Time: 20-30 minutes
Serves: 8

INGREDIENTS

2lbs potatoes, peeled and quartered
Water to cover
¼ tsp salt
2 cups hot milk
2 tbsps butter

Pinch white pepper
Pinch salt

METHOD

Place the potatoes in a large pot, cover with water and add the ¼ tsp of salt. Cover the pot and bring to the boil. Cook about 20-25 minutes, or until tender. Drain well and return to the pot. Turn up the heat and mash the potatoes. When dry, add the hot milk and butter, beating it in well. Season with salt and pepper.

SQUASH PIE WITH WALNUT TOPPING

This is delicious change from the traditional pumpkin pie.

Preparation Time: 25 minutes
Cooking Time: 1 hour 45 minutes
Oven Temperature: 350°F
Makes: 1 10-inch pie

INGREDIENTS

Favorite recipe for a 10-inch 1-crust pastry shell

FILLING

2 cups puréed butternut squash
2 whole eggs, beaten
1 cup sugar
¾ cup milk
½ cup heavy cream
¼ tsp salt
½ tsp each ginger, nutmeg, cinnamon and allspice
1 tsp grated lemon rind
1 tsp lemon juice
4oz butter, melted and cooled

WALNUT TOPPING

3 tbsps brown sugar
2 tbsps butter
1 tbsp milk
½ cup chopped walnuts

Overleaf: Traditional Thanksgiving Dinner.

METHOD

Mix all the filling ingredients together well and pour into the unbaked prepared pie shell. Bake until a skewer inserted into the center of the filling comes out clean, about 1 hour 45 minutes. Before the pie cools, combine the topping ingredients and melt over gentle heat. Spoon over the pie and allow to cool completely before cutting to serve.

CRANBERRY PUDDING

This is a steamed pudding in the English tradition, made American by the use of cranberries and brought up-to-date by the addition of wheatgerm and honey.

Preparation Time: 25 minutes
Cooking Time: 1½ hours
Serves: 8

INGREDIENTS

1½ cups sliced cranberries
3 tbsps sugar
1½ cups whole-wheat flour
2 tsps baking powder
½ tsp salt
1 tbsp milk powder
¼ cup wheatgerm
2 eggs, well beaten
½ cup honey
⅓ cup milk

LEMON SAUCE

½ cup sugar
3 tsps cornstarch
1 cup boiling water
Juice and rind of 1 lemon
1 tbsp butter

METHOD

Place the cranberries and sugar in a bowl and leave to stand. Place all the dry ingredients in a large bowl and mix the liquid ingredients separately. Gradually add the liquid ingredients to the dry ingredients, stirring well. Fold in the cranberries and spoon into a well greased 2 pint pudding bowl or pudding basin. Cover with a sheet of wax paper and then seal the bowl or basin well with foil or a lid. Place on a rack in a pan of simmering water. Cover the pan and steam for 1½ hours.

Check the level of the water occasionally and add more water if necessary.

Meanwhile, prepare the lemon sauce. Mix the sugar and cornstarch together in a saucepan and stir in the boiling water gradually. Add the rind and juice of the lemon and bring to the boil. Stir constantly until thickened and cleared. Beat in the butter and serve warm with the pudding. If preparing the sauce in advance, place a sheet of wax paper or plastic film directly over the sauce to prevent a skin forming on the surface.

CRANBERRY MOUSSE

Like a cool, pink cloud, this dessert makes a light and lovely ending to a rich meal.

Preparation Time: 30 minutes
Cooking Time: 10 minutes
Serves: 8

INGREDIENTS

1 quart cranberries
1½ cups sugar
6oz water
1½ tsp gelatine
Juice of 1 lemon
2 tsps orange juice
1½ cups heavy cream
1 tsp vanilla extract
3 tbsps sugar

GARNISH

Whipped cream

METHOD

Combine the cranberries, sugar and water in a heavy-based saucepan and bring to the boil. Cook until soft and then purée. Meanwhile, sprinkle the gelatine on top of the lemon and orange juice and leave to soak 5 minutes. Melt over gentle heat and pour into the cranberry purée. Cool in a bowl over ice, stirring frequently until the gelatine just begins to set. Meanwhile, whip the cream and add the vanilla extract and sugar. When the mixture has reached setting point, fold in the cream and pour into individual glasses to serve. Chill until set and serve with whipped cream.

Facing page: Cranberry Pudding.

CRANBERRY NUT BREAD

Sassamanesh was the peculiar sounding Indian name for the delicious and versatile cranberry.

Preparation Time: 20 minutes
Cooking Time: 1 hour
Oven Temperature: 325°F
Makes: 1 loaf

INGREDIENTS

2 cups flour
2 tsp baking powder
1 cup sugar
½ tsp salt
1 tsp baking soda
½ cup orange juice
2 tbsps shortening, melted and cooled
4 tbsps water
1 whole egg
1½ cups chopped cranberries
½ cup chopped walnuts

METHOD

Sift the dry ingredients into a large bowl. Combine the orange juice, shortening, water and egg and stir gradually into the dry ingredients. Fold the chopped cranberries and walnuts into the batter and pour into a greased and floured 9″ x 5″ x 2¾″ bread pan. Bake for 1 hour, or until a skewer inserted into the center comes out clean.

CRANBERRY WALNUT PIE

Colonial cooks often made cranberry tarts, so this would not be out of place at a Thanksgiving celebration.

Preparation Time: 25 minutes
Cooking Time: 1 hour
Oven Temperature: 400°F reduced to 350°F
Makes: 1 10-inch pie

INGREDIENTS

Favorite recipe for 10-inch 1-crust pasty shell

Left: Cranberry Nut Bread (top) and Cranberry Walnut Pie (bottom).

FILLING

6 Granny Smith apples, peeled, cored and sliced
3 cups cranberries, roughly chopped
½ cup sugar
1 tsp cinnamon
¼ tsp nutmeg
¼ cup flour
1 cup walnuts, chopped
Pinch salt

METHOD

Combine all the filling ingredients and mix thoroughly. Spoon into the unbaked pie shell. Bake for 15 minutes at 400°F. Reduce the heat to 350°F and bake an additional 45 minutes. Serve warm.

ALL THE PRECEDING THANKSGIVING RECIPES WERE PREPARED BY ROBERT T. ALLAN, ASSISTANT EXECUTIVE CHEF, SHERATON PLYMOUTH INN, PLYMOUTH, MA

MONTEREY CHEVRE DRESSING

With the help of a food processor, this is a quickly-made salad dressing. Prepare it well ahead of time for all the flavors to blend, and serve it with your favorite salad greens. It is also delicious with sliced tomatoes or spooned on top of a ripe avocado.

Preparation Time: 10 minutes
Makes: 3 cups

INGREDIENTS

1 bunch scallions, washed
¼ cup diced onion
6oz garlic and chive Chevre cheese (room temperature)
½ cup sour cream
½ cup mayonnaise
1 cup half and half

METHOD

Cut the root ends off the scallions and chop the white portion and green tops into small pieces. Purée in a food processor

Facing page: Village Inn Harvest Vegetable Soup and side salad served with Monterey Chevre Dressing.

with the onion. Put the purée into a bowl with the cheese, sour cream and mayonnaise. Mix together well with a wire whisk, making sure the cheese is broken up and not lumpy. Beat in the half and half until the dressing is smooth and creamy. Add salt and pepper to taste, if desired. Cover and refrigerate until ready to serve. The dressing will thicken up considerably in the refrigerator, so thin with additional half and half if necessary.

CHEF JAMES E. LOWE,
THE VILLAGE INN,
LENOX, MA

VILLAGE INN HARVEST VEGETABLE SOUP

Soup was one of the mainstays of early American diets. This recipe is typical of the soups served in country villages when stock pots were kept going on the back of the stove all the time, and when villagers' own gardens provided the vegetables in the late summer and fall.

Preparation Time: 25 minutes
Cooking Time: 22 minutes
Serves: 8

INGREDIENTS

3 cups strong veal stock
3 cups strong chicken stock
½ tsp basil leaves
½ tsp thyme leaves
1 bay leaf
¼ tsp minced garlic
¼ cup diced mushrooms
¼ cup clean chopped spinach
2 tbsps tomato paste
¼ cup diced zucchini
¼ cup diced summer squash
½ cup diced onions
¼ cup diced carrots
¼ cup diced celery
¼ cup broccoli flowerets
¼ cup diced cabbage
¼ cup diced cauliflower flowerets
3 tbsps butter

METHOD

In a large stock pot, melt the butter and add the herbs, garlic,

celery and carrots. Stir well and cook until the vegetables are beginning to soften but not browning. Add the onion, broccoli and cauliflower. Stir well and cook for 2 minutes. Add the zucchini, summer squash and mushrooms and cook for a further 2 minutes. Add the spinach and cabbage and mix well. Pour in the veal stock and chicken stock and add the tomato paste. Bring to the boil and stir occasionally. Reduce the heat and let the soup simmer for 20 minutes. Remove from the heat and add salt and pepper to taste. Let the soup cool to room temperature, cover and refrigerate overnight. The fat will rise to the surface and solidify, making it easy to remove. Spoon off the hardened fat and bring the soup back to the boil. Use your favorite garnish, such as grated cheese, crôutons, or chopped parsley. Reheating and serving the soup the next day gives the flavors a chance to meld together.

CHEF JAMES E. LOWE,
THE VILLAGE INN,
LENOX, MA

AUTUMN BISQUE

Butternut squash and apples are at their best in the fall. They were both staple foods grown by the settlers for their keeping qualities. They complement one another well and taste delicious in a smooth, creamy soup.

Preparation Time: 25 minutes
Cooking Time: 40-50 minutes
Serves: 4-6

INGREDIENTS

*1 small butternut squash, unpeeled, halved and seeded
(approximately 1lb in weight)
2 green apples, peeled, cored and chopped
1 medium onion, peeled and chopped
Pinch rosemary
Pinch marjoram
1 quart chicken stock
2 slices white bread, trimmed and cubed
1½ tsps salt
¼ tsp pepper
2 egg yolks
¼ cup heavy cream*

METHOD

Combine the squash, apples, onion, herbs, stock, bread cubes, salt and pepper in a heavy saucepan. Bring to the boil and simmer, uncovered, for 30-45 minutes. Take out the squash with a draining spoon and scoop out the flesh,

discarding the skins. Return the pulp to the soup. Purée the soup in a blender or food processor until smooth and return to the rinsed out saucepan. In a small bowl, beat the egg yolks and cream together. Beat in a little of the hot soup and then stir back into the saucepan with the rest of the soup. Cook gently, stirring constantly until thickened. Do not allow the soup to boil or the eggs will curdle. Serve immediately.

CHEF STEPHEN MONGEON,
THE RED LION INN, STOCKBRIDGE, MA

CREAM OF TOMATO AND CHEDDAR SOUP

Tomato soup used to be one of the more fashionable soups for a company dinner. Cheddar cheese used to be made in every state where there was a dairy industry and was a popular food across the country. With tomatoes and cheese being such a good combination, it was natural to bring them together in one delicious soup.

Preparation Time: 25 minutes
Cooking Time: 1 hour 10 minutes
Serves: 12

INGREDIENTS

*1 small onion, chopped
4 stalks celery, leaves removed
3 carrots, peeled
2lbs canned Italian plum tomatoes
3 tbsps whole mixed pickling spice tied in a small
cheesecloth bag
4 tbsps extra virgin olive oil
1 tsp Worcestershire sauce
¼ tsp Tabasco
2 quarts veal stock
¾-1lb. Vermont Cheddar cheese double aged (4 years)
if possible, and shredded
5oz butter
5oz flour
8oz butter
1 cup heavy cream
Salt and black pepper to taste*

Previous pages: Old-Fashioned Split Pea Soup with Ham (top left), Autumn Bisque (top right) and Cream of Tomato and Cheddar Soup (bottom). Facing page: Oysters.

METHOD

Chop the onions, celery and carrots finely. Sauté in the olive oil in a 1 gallon soup pot until slightly softened. Add the tomatoes, bag of spices, Worcestershire sauce and Tabasco and simmer for 1 hour, stirring often. Remove the spice bag and purée mixture in a food processor or food mill until smooth. Return to the rinsed out pan, add the veal stock and return the spice bag to the soup. Bring to the boil, reduce the heat and simmer until reduced by about a quarter. Put 5oz butter in a small saucepan and stir in the flour. Cook over low heat for 5 minutes, but do not brown. Gradually beat the roux into the soup and bring to the boil. Simmer for 10 minutes, add Cheddar cheese, remaining butter and cream. Adjust the seasonings and serve immediately. Garnish with crôutons, additional Cheddar cheese or chopped parsley, if desired.

CHEF STEPHEN MONGEON,
THE RED LION INN, STOCKBRIDGE, MA

CAPE SCALLOP BROCHETTE

Scallops were said to be the emblem of the pilgrims who visited the shrine of St. James in Compostella. They were given scallops to eat as a penance, surely not an unpleasant one! Sea scallops are usually quite large, so cut them in half, if necessary, so that they cook in the same time as the vegetables.

Preparation Time: 20 minutes
Cooking Time: 10-15 minutes
Serves: 4

INGREDIENTS

1¼lbs fresh sea scallops
16 cherry tomatoes
8 large mushrooms
1 large green pepper, cut in large pieces
1 onion, cut in quarters
12 bacon slices

MARINADE

¾ cup vegetable oil
¼ cup wine vinegar

Right: Cape Scallop Brochette.

1 clove garlic, crushed
Pinch oregano
Pinch basil
Pinch parsley

METHOD

Wrap the scallops in the bacon. Separate the layers of onions and alternate on skewers with the scallops in bacon and the other vegetables. Mix the marinade ingredients together and brush over the brochettes. Broil on hot coals or under a preheated broiler, basting frequently with the marinade for about 10-15 minutes, or until the scallops are cooked and the bacon is crisp.

MARSHA HELLER, CHEF,
CANDLELIGHT INN, MA

OLD-FASHIONED SPLIT PEA SOUP WITH HAM

This soup is a favorite all over the country, but the addition of a ham bone is particularly New England-style. Garnishes such as crôutons, bacon bits or chopped parsley lend added interest to this soup. The addition of crusty bread and a salad creates a wonderful, hearty repast.

Preparation Time: 30 minutes plus overnight soaking
Cooking Time: 1½-2 hours
Serves: 8

INGREDIENTS

1lb dried, green split peas
2½ quarts water
2lbs ham hocks or a meaty ham bone
¼lb onion, diced
¼lb carrots, peeled and diced
¼lb celery hearts and leaves, finely diced
2 tbsps bacon or pork renderings
2 medium bay leaves
2 whole cloves
3 whole black peppercorns
½ tsp garlic powder
½ tsp thyme
1 tsp Worcestershire sauce
⅛ tsp Tabasco sauce
1lb potatoes, peeled and diced (optional)
Salt and freshly ground black pepper to taste

METHOD

Wash the peas and pick over. Soak in 2½ quarts warm water for 6-8 hours or overnight. Melt the renderings until hot in a large soup pot. Add the onion, carrots, celery, thyme, garlic powder, Worcestershire sauce and Tabasco. Sauté 3-5 minutes or until the vegetables are cooked yet still firm. Place the bay leaves, cloves and peppercorns in a square of cheesecloth and tie to make a small bag. Add the peas and soaking liquid, ham hocks or bone and the cheesecloth bag to the pan and bring the mixture to the boil. Skim off the foam when the mixture comes to the boil. Reduce the heat and simmer gently for 1½ hours. Add the diced potato at this time, if desired, and simmer an additional 30 minutes. Remove the ham hocks or bone and set aside to cool. Remove the meat and discard any fat, sinew and gristle. Dice the lean meat into small cubes. Check the consistency of the soup and, if desired, add more water. If the soup is not thick enough, extend the cooking time. Add the diced ham, adjust the seasonings and serve with the desired garnishes or accompaniments.

CHEF STEPHEN MONGEON,
THE RED LION INN,
STOCKBRIDGE, MA

OYSTERS ROCKEFELLER

This recipe has become a classic. It makes a luxurious first course, especially with the price of oysters! Perhaps that is why it carries the name of one of the wealthiest families in the United States.

Preparation Time: 25 minutes
Cooking Time: 12-15 minutes
Oven Temperature: 350°F
Makes: 6 oysters

INGREDIENTS

1lb fresh spinach or ½lb frozen chopped spinach
6 oysters on the half shell
½ cup grated cheese

FISH VELOUTÉ SAUCE

1½ tbsps butter
1½ tbsps flour
Pinch salt and white pepper
½ cup fish stock or clam juice
2 tsps Poupon mustard

METHOD

If using fresh spinach, wash well and remove any thick stalks. Place in a saucepan with a tight-fitting lid with a pinch of salt. Cook just until the leaves begin to wilt, remove from the heat, drain and press in a colander to remove all the water. Chop by hand or in a food processor and return to the pan over heat. Cook for 1 minute to evaporate any remaining liquid. If using frozen spinach, do not re-cook. Drain it very well and place in the pan for 1 minute over heat to dry. To prepare the sauce, melt the butter in a small saucepan and stir in the flour. Cook for 1-2 minutes, stirring constantly until a pale straw color. Gradually whisk in the stock, add salt and pepper and bring back to the boil. Allow to simmer 1-2 minutes or until thickened. Combine with the mustard and stir into the spinach. Spoon the spinach mixture on top of each oyster and sprinkle on the greated cheese. Bake in a moderate oven for 10-12 minutes and heat through to melt the cheese. Alternatively, top the spinach with Hollandaise sauce.

UNION OYSTER HOUSE,
BOSTON, MA

Above, from left: Clams Casino, Oysters Rockefeller and Baked Stuffed Cherrystones. Overleaf: Lobster Thermidor.

BAKED STUFFED CHERRYSTONES

Cherrystones are hard-shelled clams found in abundance off the coast of Massachusetts and all along the Eastern seaboard. Filled with a flavorful stuffing, they make a delicious first course.

Preparation Time: 25 minutes
Cooking Time: 10-12 minutes
Oven Temperature: 350°F
Makes: 6 stuffed clams

INGREDIENTS

6 tbsps butter or margarine
2 tbsps diced onion

2 tbsps diced green pepper
6 mushrooms, thinly sliced
Pinch dry mustard
Pinch garlic powder
¼ tsp oregano
2 tbsps clam juice
4 tbsps water
Bread crumbs
6 cherrystone clams on the half shell

METHOD

Put the butter in a small pan and sauté the onions, peppers and mushrooms until done. Add mustard, garlic, oregano and a pinch of salt and pepper. Stir in the water and the clam juice and bring to the boil. Remove from the heat and add enough bread crumbs to bring the mixture together. Allow it to cool and spoon the mixture on the clams. Bake in their shells for 10-12 minutes in a moderate oven.

UNION OYSTER HOUSE,
BOSTON, MA

BAKED BOSTON SCROD

Scrod is a term for a young codfish weighing about 2lbs or under, but it may also refer to the same size pollock or haddock. Cod was one of the mainstays of the colonists' diet and gave its name to America's best-known cape. This method of preparing scrod is famous all over the country.

Preparation Time: 15 minutes
Cooking Time: 10 minutes
Oven Temperature: 400°F
Serves: 1-2

INGREDIENTS

8oz fresh baby cod
Fresh lemon juice
White wine
Coarse bread crumbs
Chopped parsley
Paprika
Garlic powder
Onion powder
Salt and pepper
Melted butter

METHOD

Sprinkle the cod with fresh lemon juice and a little white wine. Mix the crumbs with the remaining ingredients except the melted butter and sprinkle on top of the fish to coat the top thickly. Drizzle with melted butter and bake for about 10 minutes, or until the fish flakes easily.

MARSHA HELLER, CHEF,
CANDLELIGHT INN, MA

LOBSTER THERMIDOR

Lobsters were common fare for the Pilgrims even though they have now become a luxury. American or Northern lobsters live only on the Eastern coast of North America and thrive in the cold water. Be sure to choose a lobster which is heavy in weight in proportion to its size. This indicates that it will be a meaty and well flavored one.

Preparation Time: 40 minutes
Cooking Time: 25 minutes
Serves: 1

INGREDIENTS

1¼lb whole cooked lobster
¾ cup heavy cream
1 egg yolk
Salt and pepper
Pinch cayenne pepper
1 tbsp sherry
½ a small green pepper, sliced
½ a small red pimento, sliced
1oz sliced mushrooms
1 tbsp Dijon mustard

HOLLANDAISE SAUCE

1 egg yolk
2oz butter, melted
Dash lemon juice
Pinch salt and pepper
2 tbsps grated cheese

Facing page: Baked Boston Scrod.

GARNISH

Black olives
Mashed potato
Lemon wedges

METHOD

Cut the lobster in half lengthwise and loosen the tail meat but do not remove. Crack the large claws and remove all the meat. Remove the legs and extract as much meat as possible from them. Clean out the body cavity of the lobster. (The green tomally or liver may be eaten, as can the roe or coral.) Pour the heavy cream into a small saucepan and bring to the boil. Add salt, pepper and sherry and reduce the cream by a ¼. Beat the egg yolks and beat in a spoonful of the hot cream. Pour the egg yolks into the cream in the saucepan and cook over gentle heat, stirring continuously until it just coats the back of a spoon. Sauté the peppers, pimentos and mushrooms in about 1 tbsp of butter until cooked. Add the lobster claw meat and any meat from the legs to the vegetables and stir in the mustard. Pour on the sauce and keep warm.

Meanwhile, prepare the Hollandaise sauce. Place the egg yolk and the lemon juice and a pinch of salt and pepper in a blender. Heat the butter until bubbling and, with the machine running, pour the butter in through the funnel gradually. Set the sauce aside. To assemble, pipe a border of the mashed potatoes on a large ovenproof plate and brown under a preheated broiler. Place the lobster, cut side up, in the center of the potato border. Spoon the thermidor sauce into the body cavity and coat some over the tail. Spoon the Hollandaise sauce on top of the thermidor sauce and sprinkle with grated cheese. Place in the oven or under the broiler until golden brown on top. Decorate the potato border with lemons and olives and serve immediately.

UNION OYSTER HOUSE,
BOSTON, MA

SHRIMP SCAMPI CANDLELIGHT

Scampi are not really shrimp but Dublin Bay Prawns or langoustines, which were once plentiful in the Bay of Naples. These shellfish are not native to American waters although shrimp, prepared in one of the same ways as scampi, makes a delicious substitute.

Left: Shrimp Scampi Candlelight.

Preparation Time: 15 minutes
Cooking Time: 8-10 minutes
Oven Temperature: 400°F
Serves: 4

INGREDIENTS

16 large shrimp, cut down the middle, cleaned and left in their shells

SAUCE

8oz butter, melted
2 cloves garlic, crushed
2 tbsps tarragon, chopped
2 tsps Dijon mustard
Dash A-1 sauce
Dash Worcestershire sauce
Dash Tabasco
Dash red wine vinegar
1 large tbsp sour cream
Dash lemon juice

METHOD

Place the shrimp in an ovenproof dish and combine all the sauce ingredients. Beat well and pour over the shrimp. Cook for 8-10 minutes, or until the shrimp shells turn pink.

MARSHA HELLER, CHEF,
CANDLELIGHT INN, MA

MUSSELS BASQUE STYLE

One of the tastiest shellfish to be found off the Massachusetts coast is the mussel. The best mussels grow in the tidal channels, where they are covered by water 24 hours a day.

Preparation Time: 25 minutes
Cooking Time: 5-6 minutes
Serves: 4 as an appetizer or 2 as a main course

INGREDIENTS

1¼ lbs mussels, well scrubbed
1 cup clam juice
1 large clove garlic, chopped
½ cup white wine
2 tbsps chopped onion
2 tbsps chopped parsley

METHOD

Discard any mussels that do not open when their shells are tapped or those that have broken shells. Place the mussels and all the other ingredients in a 2 quart saucepan. Cover the pan and cook until the mussels open, about 5-6 minutes. Stir the mussels occasionally while cooking. Pour into a large bowl or crock to serve. Accompany with garlic bread.

UNION OYSTER HOUSE,
BOSTON, MA

CLAMS CASINO

There have been many different versions of this delicious clam dish, but green pepper and bacon are two of the original ingredients. Oysters can be cooked in the same way.

Preparation Time: 25 minutes
Cooking Time: 5-7 minutes
Oven Temperature: 350°F
Makes: 6 stuffed clams

INGREDIENTS

½ cup butter or margarine
½oz diced green pepper
½oz diced red pepper or pimento
½oz diced onion
2-3 drops Tabasco sauce
¼ tsp Worcestershire sauce
3 slices bacon

METHOD

Place the butter, peppers, pimento and onion in a mixing bowl and blend thoroughly by hand until the butter is softened and all the ingredients are incorporated. Mix in the Tabasco and Worcestershire sauce. Slice the bacon in half and set it aside. Spoon the butter mixture on top of the clams and place a half slice of bacon on top. Bake in a moderate oven for approximately 5-7 minutes, or until heated through and the bacon is crisp.

UNION OYSTER HOUSE,
BOSTON, MA

Facing page: Mussels Basque Style (top), Bouillabaisse (right), Oyster House Clam Chowder (center) and Seafood Primavera (bottom left).

SEAFOOD PRIMAVERA

Primavera means springtime. The name is usually applied to a pasta dish containing tender, colorful vegetables. Since shellfish, especially lobster, is so plentiful and good in Massachusetts, it is a natural choice to include in this dish.

Preparation Time: 35 minutes
Cooking Time: 15-20 minutes
Serves: 1

INGREDIENTS

1½oz lobster meat (tail and claws)
3oz small shrimp
2oz sea scallops
1oz sliced zucchini
1oz sliced carrots
1½oz broccoli flowerets
1½oz green peas
4oz linguine (or other noodles)
1oz canned tomato sauce
Fish Velouté (see recipe for Oysters Rockerfeller)
2 tbsps oil
1 clove garlic, chopped

METHOD

Place the oil and garlic in a sauté pan and cook the carrots and broccoli for a few minutes. Add the zucchini, peas and mushrooms and sauté briefly. Add the shrimp, scallops and lobster and cook until well done. Set aside and prepare the fish velouté. When the sauce is finished, mix it with the tomato sauce and add to the vegetables and seafood, tossing to coat. Cook the linguine until al dente, drain well and place on a large platter. Spoon the shellfish, vegetables and sauce on top of the linguine and sprinkle with chopped parsley, if desired. Serve immediately.

UNION OYSTER HOUSE,
BOSTON, MA

BOUILLABAISSE

This classic Provençal fish stew is an ideal recipe for using Boston's delicious seafood.

Preparation Time: 30 minutes
Cooking Time: 30 minutes
Serves: 2

INGREDIENTS

STOCK MIXTURE

1 medium carrot
1 small bunch leeks, well washed
1 medium onion
6 tbsps butter
1 8oz can whole tomatoes
Pinch saffron
1 small clove garlic, chopped
1 gallon fish stock
⅓ cup white wine

SEAFOOD

1 lobster
12oz whitefish (halibut or cod)
12-16 mussels, well scrubbed
20-24 steamers or littlenecks (clams)
½lb scallops
6 large shrimp, peeled and de-veined
12 tiny whole potatoes (canned or fresh)

METHOD

Cut the carrot, onion and leeks into julienne strips 1-2 inches long. Melt the butter in a sauté pan and add the garlic. Sauté the vegetable strips until nearly done. Add the saffron and white wine and simmer for 5 minutes. Break up the tomatoes and add to the mixture. Simmer for 5 minutes and add the fish stock. Bring to the boil, remove from the heat and allow to cool. Place all of the shellfish, except the shrimp, in a large pot. Add the cooled stock mixture and bring back to the boil. Allow to simmer gently about 20 minutes, or until the lobster is done. Remove from the heat and add the shrimp. Leave to stand, covered, for approximately 3-5 minutes. Remove the lobster and quarter it. Serve half a lobster tail and one large claw per person. Divide the smaller legs between the two servings. Divide the rest of the fish and shellfish between two crocks or soup bowls and ladle over some of the stock. Serve with garlic bread.

UNION OYSTER HOUSE,
BOSTON, MA

OYSTER HOUSE CLAM CHOWDER

When Americans think of clam chowder they think of Boston,

and the Union Oyster House is one of the most famous places to serve it. It is usually accompanied by oyster or pilot crackers.

Preparation Time: 30 minutes
Cooking Time: 35-40 minutes
Serves: 10

INGREDIENTS

2lbs potatoes, peeled and diced
4lbs fresh or frozen clams, shelled and diced
¼lb salt pork, diced
2 small onions, diced
1 cup butter
1 cup flour
10 cups clam juice
2 pints half and half
Salt and pepper
Dash Tabasco
Dash Worcestershire sauce

METHOD

Bring the potatoes and the clam juice to the boil. Cook until the potatoes are tender, about 10-15 minutes. Add the clams and any of their liquid. Cook about 5 minutes. Set aside. Add the pork to a sauté pan and cook over low heat until rendered. Add the onions and cook until transparent. Add the butter and allow it to melt. Add the flour and cook until slightly colored. Add a bit more flour if necessary if the mixture is too soft. Bring the clams, juice and potatoes back to the boil. Gradually stir in the cooked roux. Bring to a rolling boil to thicken. Stir continuously while cooking. Beat the half and half and add to the soup. It may not be necessary to use all the half and half; the soup should be thick. Adjust the seasoning and add a dash of Tabasco and Worcestershire sauce before serving.

UNION OYSTER HOUSE,
BOSTON, MA

SEIKH KEBAB

These lamb kebabs are great cooked on the outdoor grill. In case of rain, though, they can be cooked very well under a broiler. Either way, they are sure to please.

Preparation Time: 20 minutes

Cooking Time: 8-10 minutes
Serves: 6-8

INGREDIENTS

10oz raw lamb, ground
1 onion, minced
1 clove garlic, finely chopped
¼ tsp chopped fresh ginger
½ tsp garam masala
1 tsp lemon juice
1 tbsp chickpea or cornflour
¼-½ pint plain yogurt

METHOD

Make sure the lamb is finely ground. Add the onion and all the remaining ingredients except the yogurt. Knead on a pastry board like bread dough. Shape onto skewers in sausage shapes. Baste with the plain yogurt and place under a broiler or over hot coals. Baste and turn as they cook. When well done, they will come off the skewers easily. Serve with the remaining yogurt, if desired.

ROBERT T. ALLAN
ASSISTANT EXECUTIVE CHEF,
SHERATON PLYMOUTH INN, PLYMOUTH, MA

ROAST DUCKLING WITH CRANBERRIES, ORANGES AND MINT

This is an elegant recipe for duckling from a restaurant on Beacon Hill, Boston's most fashionable area. Beacon Hill is also one of the oldest residential areas in Boston and maintains its charm to this day.

Preparation Time: 30 minutes
Cooking Time: 1½-1¾ hours
Oven Temperature: 425°F
Serves: 3-4

INGREDIENTS

1 whole fresh duckling, 4-5lbs in weight
¾ cup dry sherry
¼ cup soy sauce
1lb cranberries

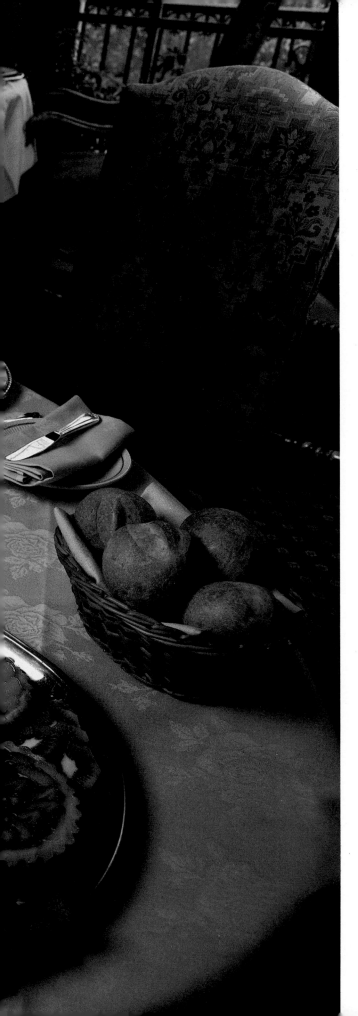

3 tbsps butter
Sugar to taste

SAUCE

4 cups good veal stock
1 cup dry sherry
1 tbsp finely chopped shallots
3 tbsps butter
3 tbsps flour
2 bunches fresh mint, washed and chopped

GARNISH

Sliced oranges
Fresh mint

METHOD

Remove the giblets from the duck and cut off the wing tips. Prick the skin all over with a sharp knife. Combine the sherry and soy sauce and pour over the duck to marinate, uncovered, for 24 hours in the refrigerator. Place one oven rack in the center of a preheated oven. Adjust the second rack in the lower third of the oven. Place on it a large pan filled with ½ inch of water. Pat the duck dry and place directly on the upper oven rack so that drippings will fall into the pan of water below. Cook until the legs move freely in their joints and the drippings in the cavity are clear.

To prepare the sauce, melt the butter in a saucepan and cook the shallots until translucent. Add the flour and cook 3-4 minutes, stirring constantly. Reduce the veal stock and the sherry to about ⅓ and stir into the flour and butter roux. Allow to boil until slightly thickened and remove from the heat. Add the mint and allow to stand for 10 minutes. Strain and season with salt and pepper and keep it warm. To finish, heat the remaining 3 tbsps butter in a deep saucepan and add the cranberries. Reduce the heat and allow the cranberries to cook briefly until just softened but not breaking up. Stir in sugar to taste and, when the duck is cooked, fill the cavity with the cooked cranberries. Line a warm serving platter with sliced oranges and place the duck on top. Pour the sauce over the duck and garnish with bunches of fresh mint.

NEAL SOLOMON, EXECUTIVE CHEF,
HAMPSHIRE HOUSE,
BEACON STREET, BOSTON, MA

Left: Roast Duckling with Cranberries Oranges and Mint, Scallop and Avocado Seviche and Fresh Fruit Tartes.

SCALLOP AND AVOCADO SEVICHE

The scallops in this recipe "cook" in the refrigerator! This dish is simple to prepare and makes a delicious first course. It will keep for 1 week in the refrigerator if stirred daily.

Preparation Time: 20 minutes plus 36-48 hours in
the refrigerator
Serves: 6

INGREDIENTS

2lbs scallops, sliced
Juice of 5 limes
1 cup salad oil
2 tomatoes, peeled, seeded and diced
2 green peppers, diced
1 avocado, diced
½ Spanish onion, minced
2 cloves garlic, crushed
¾ tsp cayenne pepper
1 tbsp white vinegar
1 tsp salt

METHOD

Combine all the ingredients and refrigerate. Cover the bowl and allow to marinate 36-48 hours, or until the scallops are opaque all the way through. Stir the seviche daily. Serve on lettuce leaves on individual plates.

NEAL SOLOMON, EXECUTIVE CHEF,
HAMPSHIRE HOUSE,
BEACON STREET, BOSTON, MA

FRESH FRUIT TARTES

This is a recipe in the true European tradition of pastry shops, reflecting America's diverse culinary heritage.

Preparation Time: 40 minutes
Cooking Time: 25-35 minutes
Oven Temperature: 425°F
reduced to 375°F
Makes: 1 11 inch tarte, 2 8 inch tartes or 6 4 inch
tartes

INGREDIENTS

PASTRY

6oz unsalted butter
3¾oz granulated sugar
2 egg yolks
¼ tsp almond extract
½ tsp vanilla extract
1½ tbsps rum with enough water to make a ¼ cup
10oz (approximately 2 cups) all-purpose flour

PASTRY CREAM

1 quart milk
1 cup sugar
5 tbsps cornstarch
4 whole eggs
2oz unsalted butter
2 tbsps vanilla extract

GLAZE

1 cup apricot jam, sieved
1 strip lemon peel
Water

TOPPING

Seasonal fruit

METHOD

To make the pastry, cream the butter and sugar together well until pale and fluffy. This may be done in a food processor or with an electric mixer. Mix all the liquid ingredients together, including the eggs, and gradually add to the butter and sugar mixture. Add the flour and blend just until all the ingredients are incorporated. Do not over-mix or the pastry will become tough. Shape the pastry into a rectangle of approximately 3″ x 5″ and wrap in plastic wrap. Place in the refrigerator to rest for 2 hours.

Meanwhile, make the pastry cream. Pour the milk into a heavy based saucepan and add approximately ⅓ of the sugar. Place over a high heat and stir until the sugar dissolves. Mix carefully to make sure the milk does not boil over. Combine the cornstarch with the remaining sugar in a bowl, mixing it well. Add the eggs to the cornstarch-sugar mixture and mix well with a wire whisk. When the milk begins to boil and

Facing page: Roast Duckling with Cranberries, Oranges and Mint. Overleaf: Roast Prime Ribs of Beef Red Lion.

froth, turn off the heat. Add a bit of the hot milk to the egg and sugar mixture and then pour it into the saucepan and stir constantly. Lower the heat to medium and bring the mixture slowly to the boil. Stir continuously and cook for 2 minutes. Take off the heat and add the butter in pieces, making sure it covers the entire surface of the cream when melted. When the pastry cream is fairly cool, add the vanilla extract and stir well. Taste and add more vanilla if desired. Place immediately in a clean container and put a sheet of plastic wrap directly on the surface of the cream. Refrigerate and use within 1 week. When ready to use, whip well until smooth.

To make the tart, cut slices of dough about 16th of an inch thick and press onto the sides and bottom of a false-bottomed tart pan. Cut off any excess with a sharp knife. If the pastry becomes too soft while shaping, chill again in the refrigerator for about 20 minutes, or until firm. Fill the lined tart pan with the cooled pastry cream. Place the tart pan onto a baking sheet. Bake at 425°F for 10 minutes. Turn the pan around and lower the oven temperature to 375°F. Bake an additional 15 to 25 minutes, depending upon the size of the tart, or until the pastry is light brown and pastry cream is puffed and lightly browned. Remove from the oven and allow to cool.

Meanwhile, prepare the glaze by combining the ingredients in a small saucepan and cooking until syrupy. Allow the glaze to cool slightly. When the tart is cooled, remove the sides of the pan. Using a spatula, loosen the tart from the bottom of the pan and carefully slide it onto a clean work surface. Arrange the fruit in contrasting colors in a decorative pattern on top of the pastry cream. Brush the fruit and the entire surface of the tart, including the crust, with the warm glaze. When the glaze is set and cool, refrigerate the tart. Serve within 24 hours of final assembly.

DAVID BERGER LIMITED,
FINE EUROPEAN CAKES,
MEDFORD, MA

ROAST PRIME RIBS OF BEEF RED LION

The Red Lion in the recipe title refers to the Red Lion Inn in Stockbridge, Massachusetts, located in the picturesque Berkshire Hills. This recipe reflects the British heritage of the region.

Preparation Time: 2 hours
Cooking Time: 3-3 hours 15 minutes

Oven Temperature: as indicated in the methods
Serves: 12

INGREDIENTS

BEEF
1 7-rib, 22-24lbs Black Angus Prime Rib with fat cap
4 fl oz Worcestershire sauce

RED LION SEASONING
3½ tbsps salt
½ tbsp ground white pepper
½ tbsp ground black pepper
1 tbsp coarse garlic powder
1 tbsp leaf thyme

POPOVERS (individually prepared Yorkshire puddings)
6 large eggs
4 cups all-purpose flour
½ tsp salt
¼ tsp garlic powder
⅛ tsp ground white pepper
12 fl oz beef drippings from the roasting pan

AU JUS
2 tbsps beef drippings (from roasting the meat)
2 small onions, chopped
1 large carrot, chopped
3 stalks celery with leaves, chopped
1 pint tawny or ruby port
1 medium Spanish onion, sliced in half horizontally
2 quarts well flavored beef broth
3 whole cloves
1 clove garlic, crushed
2 bay leaves
1 tsp thyme

METHOD

Preheat the oven to 350°F for the beef. Leave the beef at room temperature for 1 hour before roasting. Prick the fat with a sharp fork and rub the top and sides thoroughly with Worcestershire sauce. Rub all of the Red Lion seasoning into the fat cap. Place the ribs in a shallow roasting pan with the fat cap facing up. Let the beef stand for an additional 2 hours at room temperature to contribute to the flavor and tenderness. Roast the beef for approximately 3 to 3¼ hours, or to an internal temperature of 120°F. Remove the roast from the pan and keep in a warm, draught-free area for 30 to 40 minutes before carving. Take out all but 2 tbsp of the drippings from the pan and reserve the remaining for popovers.

To prepare the popovers, increase the oven temperature to 450°F. Combine all the ingredients and blend slightly with a whisk. The mixture will still be slightly lumpy. Add 2 tbsps of the beef drippings to each of 12 muffin pan cups. Place the pans in the oven and heat to a smoking point. Fill the cups not more than ⅓ full with batter. Place in the oven for 10 minutes. Do not open the oven door to check for at least 10 minutes. Reduce the oven temperature to 350°F and cook an additional 15 minutes, or until the popovers are golden brown. Turn off the oven and leave the door open. Remove the popovers from the pan and place them on a warm serving platter in the oven. Add the reserved 2 tbsps of beef drippings to the roasting pan along with the chopped onions, carrot and celery. Sauté gently in the pan for 5 minutes. Add the tawny or ruby port and bring to the boil. Reduce by about ⅓. Take half of the Spanish onion and cook over an open flame and add to the pan. Add the beef broth and all the remaining ingredients. Bring to the boil, reduce slightly and strain.

To serve, place the beef on a large serving platter and garnish with oven-roasted vegetables. Serve the popovers on the side. Complement the dish by preparing a sauce-boat of horseradish cream sauce and serve with the Au Jus separately. Slice the meat, alternating between slices on the bone and slices off the bone.

CHEF STEPHEN MONGEON,
THE RED LION INN,
STOCKBRIDGE, MA

CORN BREAD

Corn and cornmeal play a very important part in Massachusetts cuisine. Without the knowledge gained from the Indians on how to plant and grow corn, the people of the Massachusetts Bay Colony probably would not have survived their first winter.

Preparation Time: 20 minutes
Cooking Time: 25 minutes
Oven Temperature: 400°F
Makes: 24 squares

INGREDIENTS

10 whole eggs
1 cup sugar
1 tbsp salt
1½ quarts milk
1lb 12oz cornmeal

1lb 10oz bread flour
3 tbsps baking powder
⅔ cup melted butter
½ tsp vanilla extract

METHOD

Beat the eggs, sugar and salt until thick. Add the milk and sift in the cornmeal, bread flour and baking powder. Add the melted butter and stir in gently. Pour into a greased 24″ x 8″ baking pan. Bake for 25 minutes or until well risen and golden brown on top. Cool on a rack and cut into squares while still warm.

UNION OYSTER HOUSE,
BOSTON, MA

ROAST QUAIL JAMES WITH MUSHROOMS AND PECAN DRESSING

Quail was always plentiful in the colonies and cooks prided themselves on serving these tiny game birds with a rich stuffing for special occasions. If the birds are young and tender, they should never be cooked more than 25 minutes.

Preparation Time: 30 minutes
Cooking Time: 27 minutes
Serves: 6

INGREDIENTS

12 whole European-style boned quail
Flour for dusting
Salt and pepper
¼ cup Madeira wine
1 cup veal stock
4 tbsps minced shallots

DRESSING
½ cup mushrooms, diced
¾ cup diced celery
¾ cup diced onion
¾ cup pecan halves
2 tbsps butter
½ cup bread crumbs
1 tsp poultry seasoning

Salt and pepper
½ tsp thyme
½ tsp basil

METHOD

First prepare the dressing. Heat the butter in a saucepan and add the mushrooms, celery and onion. Cook the vegetables until they are just tender. Add the poultry seasoning, salt, pepper, and herbs. Allow the vegetables to cool and place in a food processor with the bread crumbs and the pecans. Process until smooth and add salt and pepper to taste. Prepare the quail, cut off the wing tips and secure the front of each quail using a thin toothpick. Sew together the excess skin on the breast, sealing it completely. Fill a pastry bag with the dressing and place the tip in the opening at the back of each quail. Fill the quail with dressing, being careful not to over-fill or the quails will burst while roasting. Sew up the back opening of each quail, or pinch together with toothpicks. Sprinkle each quail with salt and pepper and dust lightly with flour. Heat about 2 tbsps butter in an ovenproof pan and brown the quails on all sides. Place them in the oven, breast side up, and roast for 25 minutes. Baste them at least 3 times with the pan juices during roasting. When they are done, place them on a hot platter and cover with foil to keep warm. To make the sauce, pour off almost all the butter, add the shallots and sauté them. Add the Madeira and flambé. Allow the wine to reduce to about 2 tbsps. Add the stock and reduce by about half. Season with salt and finish with 2 tbsps of butter swirled in off the heat. To serve the quail, put 2 on each plate and cover with about 2 tbsps of sauce. On each quail leg, put a tiny paper frill. Serve with honey glazed carrots and wild rice or any other appropriate combination.

CHEF JAMES E. LOWE,
THE VILLAGE INN,
LENOX, MA

CHICKEN POT PIE

There are many versions of this pie to be found all over the country. This recipe uses chicken especially prepared for the pie, but left-over chicken can be used as well. The topping of buttermilk biscuits makes this a real country-style pie.

Preparation Time: 35 minutes

Left: Roast Quail James with Mushrooms and Pecan Dressing. Overleaf: Chicken Pot Pie.

Cooking Time: 40-50 minutes
Serves: 6

INGREDIENTS

PIE FILLING

4 chicken breasts
1½ quarts water
½ tsp rosemary
1 clove garlic, crushed
2 bay leaves
½ tsp thyme
¼ tsp tarragon
4 whole black peppercorns
24 pearl onions
1 cup peas
2 carrots, peeled and diced
2 fl oz white wine

BISCUIT TOPPING

3½ cups all-purpose flour
1 tbsp plus 1 tsp baking powder
Good pinch salt
7 tbsps butter
1¼ cups buttermilk
Egg wash (1 whole egg and 1 tbsp water beaten until frothy)

METHOD

To prepare the filling, combine the chicken, water, wine, garlic, herbs and peppercorns in a large saucepan and bring to the boil. Skim the top and reduce the heat. Allow to simmer 20-30 minutes, or until the chicken is tender. Remove the chicken from the pot and allow it to cool. Skin and remove the meat from the bone. Return the bones to the stock. Simmer the stock until reduced by half. Strain the stock and bring back to the boil. Blend 4 tbsps of butter and 4 tbsps of flour and cook over low heat for 5 minutes without browning. Beat the stock gradually into this mixture. Simmer for 10 minutes. Cook the carrots and onions in separate pots of boiling water until tender. Dice the chicken and combine with all the remaining ingredients in individual crocks.

Meanwhile, prepare the biscuits. Preheat the oven to 400°F and combine all the dry ingredients in a bowl. Cut in the butter until the mixture has the consistency of small peas. Add the buttermilk, stirring in gradually. On a floured board, roll out the dough about ½ to ¾ inch thick. Cut with a floured biscuit cutter and brush each round with the egg wash. Bake for 25-30 minutes or until golden brown. When the biscuits are removed from the oven, brush with melted butter. Place one biscuit on top of each crock of chicken filling. Cook through in the oven until piping hot and serve immediately.

CHEF STEPHEN MONGEON,
THE RED LION INN,
STOCKBRIDGE, MA

ROAST BEEF HASH

Hash is a great way to use up left-over roast beef. It is a very versatile dish, too. Serve it for brunch, lunch or a light supper. Sauce Espagnole is an excellent one to have in your recipe file. It has so many uses.

Preparation Time: 25 minutes
Cooking Time: 25 minutes
Serves: 1

INGREDIENTS

1 medium potato, cooked
¼ onion
1 cup cooked roast beef, in large pieces
Pinch marjoram
Pinch thyme
Salt and pepper

SAUCE ESPAGNOLE

½ cup butter
2 tbsps celery, onion and carrot, minced
½ cup flour
1 quart brown stock
½ cup red wine
2 bay leaves
1 tsp thyme
½ tsp whole black peppercorns
1 tbsp tomato paste
1 egg, poached

METHOD

Put all the hash ingredients into a food processor and grind to a coarse consistency. Melt butter, dripping or oil in a large frying pan and when hot put in the hash mixture shaped into a patty. Brown on both sides until crisp on the outside.

Facing page: Roast Beef Hash.

To prepare the sauce, melt the butter in a large saucepan and sauté the mirepoix of celery, onion and carrot. When beginning to soften, add the flour and cook on high heat, scraping the bottom of the pan constantly, until the flour and vegetables are a golden brown. Gradually pour on the stock and add the remaining ingredients. Bring to the boil and cook for 20 minutes, until thickened. Strain and reserve. Serve the hash with a poached egg on top and some of the sauce poured around it.

MARSHA HELLER, CHEF,
CANDLELIGHT INN, MA

SHAKER-STYLE CHICKEN BREASTS WITH A CIDER SAUCE

The Shakers were a religious community that flourished in late 18th and early 19th century in the United States. They were dedicated to productive labour and to a life of perfection. The style of cooking was based on good, honest ingredients.

Preparation Time: 25 minutes
Cooking Time: 30 minutes
Oven Temperature: 350°F
Serves: 4

INGREDIENTS

2 whole chicken breasts with wings attached
Flour for dusting
½ cup apple cider
½ cup apple cider vinegar
2 tbsps honey
¾ cup heavy cream
1 apple, peeled, cored and diced
3 tbsps minced parsley
2 tbsps butter

METHOD

Skin and bone the chicken breasts, leaving the wings attached. Cut off the wings at the second joint and cut the breasts in half lengthwise. Salt and pepper the chicken and dust lightly with flour. Heat the butter in an ovenproof pan and brown

Right: Shaker-Style Chicken Breasts with a Cider Sauce.

the breasts skin side down first. Turn over and place the chicken breasts in the oven. Bake for about 20 minutes, or until cooked through but not dry. Remove the chicken to a hot platter and cover with foil to keep warm. Pour off almost all the fat from the pan and sauté the diced apple until golden brown. Remove the apples to drain on paper towels. Pour off any remaining liquid from the pan and add the honey and vinegar. Reduce over a medium heat until the liquid is almost a glaze, being careful not to let it boil over. Take the pan off the heat and add the apple cider slowly, stirring in gradually. Return the pan to medium heat and continue cooking to reduce by about ¾. Be careful not to let the liquid burn. Pour in the heavy cream and cook over high heat to reduce slightly. To serve, cut wings off the breasts and place them at the top center of each serving plate. Cap each wing with a paper frill. Slice the rest of the chicken breasts into thin slices, using the wing tips as the center point, and fan the chicken slices out on the plates. Divide the sauce evenly among the plates. Sprinkle the diced apple over the chicken and add some chopped parsley. Serve with quartered sautéed mushrooms or your favorite vegetable.

CHEF JAMES E. LOWE,
THE VILLAGE INN,
LENOX, MA

BOSTON BAKED BEANS

In Colonial New England there were no fast food restaurants along the highways, so it was necessary for the traveler to carry his own provisions. In the winter, it was common for housewives to line a bean crock with cloth, pour in Boston baked beans and leave the crock outside to freeze. Frozen beans were easily lifted out and carried wrapped in the cloth. When the traveler was hungry, he broke off a chunk of the beans, thawed them out over his fire and ate them for his meal.

Preparation Time: 20 minutes plus overnight soaking
for the beans
Cooking Time: 3½ hours
Oven Temperature: 300°F
Serves: 8

INGREDIENTS

1lb package navy or pea beans
¼lb salt pork, cut into 2-inch pieces
1 small whole onion, peeled
1 tsp dry mustard

6 cups water
½ tsp baking soda
⅓ cup molasses
3 tbsps sugar
1 tsp salt
¼ tsp pepper

METHOD

Soak the beans overnight in a large pot with 6 cups of water. Add the baking soda and bring to the boil. Allow to simmer 10 minutes, drain and reserve the liquid. Place the beans, salt pork and onion in a bean pot or casserole. Add the molasses, sugar, dry mustard, salt, pepper and a cup of the bean cooking liquid. Stir thoroughly and add enough liquid to cover the beans. Cover the bean pot or casserole with its lid. Bake 2 hours at 300°F. Add the remaining liquid and stir again. Bake additional 1½ hours or until the beans are tender. Uncover for the last ½ hour of cooking.

BERKSHIRE APPLE PANCAKE

These apple pancakes are similar to ones prepared in Germany and also have something in common with the French fruit and batter pudding called clafoutis.

Preparation Time: 30 minutes
Cooking Time: 25-28 minutes
Oven Temperature: 375°F reduced to 350°F
Serves: 6

INGREDIENTS

2½ cups all-purpose flour
2oz shortening
8 eggs
1 pint buttermilk
1¾ tsps salt
1¾ tsps sugar
1¾ tsps baking soda
1½ tbsps baking powder
1 tbsp vanilla extract

Facing page: Boston Baked Beans. Overleaf: Berkshire Apple Pancake.

1 tsp ground cinnamon
⅛ tsp ground nutmeg
2 tbsps melted butter
2 large MacIntosh apples, peeled, cored and diced
1 large MacIntosh apple, peeled, cored and sliced

GLAZE

6oz pure maple syrup
4 tbsps apple cider
2 tbsps melted butter
½ cup dark brown sugar

METHOD

Combine all the dry ingredients and add the shortening, eggs, buttermilk, vanilla, cinnamon, nutmeg and melted butter. With a wooden spoon, mix all the ingredients together. Do not over-mix; the mixture should look lumpy. Add the 2 diced apples and fold into the mixture. Allow to stand for 15 minutes before cooking.

Meanwhile, make the glaze. Combine the butter and cider over a low heat and add the sugar, maple syrup and mix well. Lightly brush 6½" French crêpe pans with softened butter. Heat in the oven for 3 minutes. Remove the pans from the oven and ladle in about 6 fl oz of the batter, bringing it to within a ¼ inch of the top of the pan. Decorate each pancake with 4 of the reserved apple slices. Return to the oven for a further 10 minutes. Reduce the heat to 350°F and bake for 15-18 minutes, or until a skewer comes out clean from the center when tested. Remove from the oven and allow to stand for 5 minutes. Loosen the pancake from the edges and slide out onto a warm plate. Lightly brush with glaze and serve the remaining glaze separately. Serve with fruit such as a strawberry fan or an orange twist, if desired. The pancake can also be prepared in one large skillet and sliced into wedges to serve.

CHEF STEPHEN MONGEON,
THE RED LION INN,
STOCKBRIDGE, MA

SHAKER-STYLE CHOCOLATE BREAD PUDDING WITH ENGLISH CREAM SAUCE

The Shakers derived originally from a small branch of English Quakers. There are few desserts more English than a bread pudding with a custard sauce, so it is easy to understand how, far from home, they found this dessert comforting.

Preparation Time: 20 minutes plus overnight
Cooking Time: 1 hour
Oven Temperature: 350°F
Serves: 4-6

INGREDIENTS

PUDDING

4 cups half and half
3oz semi-sweet chocolate
5 cups stale bread, cut in small dice
¾ cup brown sugar
½ tsp salt
2 tsps vanilla extract
1 cup ground walnuts
1 cup seedless raisins
5 eggs, beaten

SAUCE

2 cups milk
6 egg yolks
⅓ cup sugar
1 tsp vanilla extract

METHOD

Place the half and half in a pan with the chocolate and heat until the chocolate is melted. Stir occasionally so that the chocolate melts evenly. Combine the bread with the sugar, salt, walnuts and raisins. Mix together, breaking up any lumps of brown sugar. Add the vanilla extract and the beaten eggs and mix together well. Add the hot chocolate mixture to the bread mixture and combine thoroughly. Pour into a well-greased 8" tube pan. Place the tube pan in a larger deep pan and fill that pan with warm water until it comes halfway up the sides of the tube pan. Place the pudding in the oven for about 1 hour, or until set and firm. Test for doneness by inserting a knife into the pudding. If the blade comes out clean, the pudding is done. Let it cool, cover it and refrigerate for at least 12 hours. To unmold the pudding, let it stand in hot water for about 5 minutes and invert onto a serving platter.

To prepare the sauce, place the yolks and the sugar together and whip with a wire whisk until they are pale yellow and

Facing page: Shaker-Style Chocolate Bread Pudding with English Cream Sauce.

form ribbons. Heat the milk and vanilla extract together and bring to the boil. Gradually add the milk to the egg mixture and combine well. Pour back into the pan and place over low heat. Cook the sauce until it thickens enough to coat the back of a spoon. While the sauce is cooking, stir it constantly and do not allow it to boil. Strain through a fine sieve into a serving dish and allow to cool to room temperature. Cover and place in the refrigerator until ready to use. The sauce is best served cold.

CHEF JAMES E. LOWE,
THE VILLAGE INN,
LENOX, MA

CHOCOLATE CAKE

Long ago a clever cook discovered that chocolate combined better if melted with other ingredients, so this method of making a chocolate cake is not a new one. It is often called Devil's Food Cake for the obvious reason that it is sinfully good.

Preparation Time: 25 minutes
Cooking Time: 30-35 minutes
Oven Temperature: 350°F
Makes: 1 3 layer cake

INGREDIENTS

1½ cups milk
4 squares unsweetened chocolate
1½ cups sugar
½ cup butter
1 tsp vanilla extract
2 eggs
2 cups sifted flour
¾ tsp salt
1 tsp baking soda

ICING

5 cups sifted confectioners' sugar
Water

DECORATION

Chocolate shavings

Left: Chocolate Cake.

METHOD

Line the bottom of 13″ x 8″ x 2″ baking pan with waxed paper, then grease and flour the paper. Place 1 cup of milk, the chocolate and half a cup of sugar in the top of a double boiler. Place over boiling water and cook, stirring constantly, until the chocolate is melted. Remove from the boiling water and allow to cool. Cream the butter and remaining sugar in a large mixing bowl with an electric mixer. Add the vanilla extract and eggs and beat well. Beat in the cooled chocolate mixture. Sift the flour with the salt and add to the chocolate mixture, alternating with the remaining milk. Beat for 2 minutes on medium speed. Dissolve the soda in 3 tbsps of boiling water. Add to the cake batter and beat for 1 minute longer. Pour into the prepared pan and bake for 30-35 minutes, or until a skewer inserted into the center of the cake comes out clean. Cool in the pan for 10 minutes and then remove to a wire rack to cool completely. Trim the edge of the cake and split into 3 layers, horizontally.

To prepare the icing, sift the sugar into a large mixing bowl and stir in enough water to bring to a spreading consistency. Sandwich the layers together with the frosting and frost the top of the cake as well. Sprinkle with the shaved chocolate before the icing is completely set on top.

MARSHA HELLER, CHEF,
CANDLELIGHT INN, MA

FRESH RASPBERRIES WITH CREAM

This is a simply prepared dessert with eye-appeal and lots of flavor. Any fresh berry or combination of berries lends itself easily to this recipe.

Preparation Time: 15 minutes
Serves: 6

INGREDIENTS

*3 cups fresh raspberries or a combination
of different berries
1½ pints fresh heavy cream*

METHOD

Select the raspberries or other berries as fresh as possible. Pick over and discard bruised or damaged berries. Rinse only if absolutely necessary. Arrange the berries carefully in stemmed glass dessert dishes. Drizzle each serving with 2fl oz of heavy cream and serve.

CHEF STEPHEN MONGEON,
THE RED LION INN,
STOCKBRIDGE, MA

Facing page: Fresh Raspberries with Cream.

VERMONT

Vermont evokes images of mountain pastures with dairy cattle grazing in the crisp, fresh air, tranquil villages with white-steepled churches at their centers, and country lanes shaded by sugar maple trees brilliant with red-gold leaves in fall.

The Indians were the first people to live in this beautiful region, and the earliest European settlers were French. The name Vermont comes from the French words *vert* (green) and *mont* (mountain), and the state was so named for its thickly wooded hills. The area was opened up to further settlement after the French and Indian War, and Scottish and English settlers joined the population. Then came Irish, Italian, and Welsh immigrants. But it is surprising how many of the recipes still have a strong French background.

VERMONT

Maple syrup is synonymous with Vermont, even though this North American specialty is produced in many other states, as well as in Canada. Collecting the sap is relatively easy and does not harm the trees. Maple syrup was first produced by the Indians, and the method remained the same for at least 300 years until the 1940s, when modernization stepped in and the process lost some of its charm. The end result, though, is still delicious, and many good recipes have been developed to make use of it. Maple syrup and squash is an excellent combination. Maple syrup makes a perfect sauce for baked apples, and is a delightful substitute for molasses in baked beans, or for sugar in a quick bread. Whipped with eggs and cream, maple syrup makes a heavenly, rich mousse.

The traditional method of sap collection involves drilling holes in the trunk of the tree and gently hammering in the taps or spouts, taking care not to split the bark. Buckets are hung beneath the spouts and the sap flows each time a period of freezing is followed by a thaw. The syrup season lasts from mid-January to mid-April.

So many of the recipes that are favorites in Vermont can be traced back to French cuisine. Begin a meal in the traditional French way with pâté accompanied by cornichons – tiny pickled cucumbers. Fresh Vermont trout and crawfish make an excellent Truite au Bleu, a very French recipe. The trout is killed and quickly cleaned and cooked – a process that produces a pronounced bluish tinge on the skin of the fish.

Vermont has an abundance of game in its forests, and French country stews offer a very popular method of preparing it. Chanterelle mushrooms are also found in Vermont's wooded areas, just as in France, and adding them to a French omelet is the perfect way of using them. For dessert there is an adaptation of Tarte Tatin, a legendary apple and pastry creation.

But the food in Vermont is not exclusively French in origin. Those recipes that have become American specialties over hundreds of years, such as succotash, roast ham, and apple pie are well in evidence, and are given special touches that make them Vermont specialties as well. Vermont is proud of its heritage, and its cooks are proud of their heritage, too.

Facing page: Country Pâté

COUNTRY PÂTÉ

A scrumptious pork pâté prepared in the traditional way makes a wonderful first course and can be made two days ahead of time. The mixture can also be ground in a food processor, but don't over-work it; this pâté should be coarse-textured. Serve with French bread and cornichons.

Preparation Time: 30 minutes
Cooking Time: 4 hours
Oven Temperature: 300°F
Serves: 6

INGREDIENTS

1 pig's head (to yield 1½lbs cooked meat, cleaned)
1¼lbs pork liver
2½lbs fresh pork butt
2 medium onions
1 carrot
2 cloves garlic
2 tbsps butter
Salt and white pepper

METHOD

Purchase a cleaned pig's head from a butcher. Rinse it thoroughly and place in a large pot with enough water to cover. Add 1 of the onions and the carrot, peeled and chopped. Simmer until the meat is falling from the bones, at least 2 hours. Remove the meat from the pot and allow to cool. Remove meat from the bone and weigh out the 1½lbs needed. Meanwhile, dice the liver and pork butt. Season with salt and pepper and refrigerate for 12 hours. Dice the remaining onion and garlic cloves and sauté in the butter. Combine with all the other prepared ingredients and run the mixture through a grinding machine on medium grinding plate. Place the ground mixture in a terrine with a tightly fitting cover. Bake, covered, for about 2½ hours. Refrigerate for 48 hours before serving.

NEW ENGLAND CULINARY INSTITUTE,
MONTPELIER, VT

CABBAGE SOUP

An unusual combination, but one that uses everyday ingredients, readily available and simple to prepare. A pressure cooker will cut the cooking time by a third. This soup tastes even better when reheated the next day.

Preparation Time: 25 minutes plus overnight soaking
Cooking Time: 1 hour 50 minutes
Serves: 4-6

INGREDIENTS

2 cups dried kidney beans
3 tbsps duck or goose fat or butter
1 medium onion, thinly sliced
1 small cabbage, thinly sliced
4 cloves garlic, chopped
2 tomatoes, peeled, seeded and chopped

METHOD

Pick over and rinse the beans. Soak overnight in 2 quarts of cold water. In a heavy based pot, melt the fat or butter and cook the onion and cabbage slowly, stirring occasionally until translucent. Add the remaining ingredients, including the beans and soaking water. Bring to the boil and then simmer for 1½ hours or until the beans are tender. Check the seasoning and serve.

NEW ENGLAND CULINARY INSTITUTE,
MONTPELIER, VT

CORNICHON PICKLES

Choose the smallest possible pickling cucumbers for this recipe. Sprinkling with salt and leaving them overnight helps draw out the moisture and makes the pickles crisp. In France, these pickles are served with pâté and small pickled onions.

Preparation Time: 25 minutes plus overnight standing
Cooking Time: approximately 20 minutes
Makes: 1 quart

INGREDIENTS

12oz small pickling cucumbers
4 tbsps Kosher salt
2 cups white wine vinegar
10 whole black peppercorns
1 sprig fresh thyme
2 cloves garlic
1 chili pepper

METHOD

Rinse the cucumbers, place in a colander and sprinkle with salt. Leave to stand overnight. Drain and wipe the cucumbers with a paper towel. Sterilize a quart preserving jar, first washing it in hot, soapy water and then rinsing. Boil the jar in water to cover for 15 minutes. Place the small cucumbers in the sterilized jar with the peppercorns, thyme, garlic and chili pepper. Combine the vinegar and water in a saucepan and bring to the boil. Pour the water and vinegar over the cucumbers and spices in the jar and seal. The cornichon pickles can be served 2 weeks later.

NEW ENGLAND CULINARY INSTITUTE,
MONPELIER, VT

ROAST VERMONT TURKEY

Turkey is so closely associated with Thanksgiving that we often forget about cooking it at any other time. It's too good to limit to one day a year, and roasting a turkey is no more difficult than roasting a chicken. Try serving it with the recipe for Chestnut Stuffing.

Preparation Time: 15 minutes
Cooking Time: 3 hours
Oven Temperature: 325°F
Serves: 8-10

INGREDIENTS

1 fresh Vermont turkey, 20lbs in weight
Salt and pepper
1 onion, peeled and quartered (optional)

METHOD

Remove the giblets from the turkey and rinse thoroughly. Pat dry and season the cavity with salt and pepper. Place the turkey on a rack, breast side up, in a roasting pan. Cover the legs with foil and roast for 1-1½ hours in a preheated oven. Baste often. Remove the foil from the drumsticks and continue roasting for another 1½ hours or until the internal temperature at the thigh registers 180°F. Let rest for 20 minutes before

Right: Roast Vermont Turkey (top left), Cabbage Soup (top right), Fresh Cranberry Sauce (center), Vermont Baked Beans (bottom left) and Chestnut Stuffing (bottom right).

carving. Add the onion to the roasting pan for the last 1½ hours, if desired, to give extra flavor to the gravy.

NEW ENGLAND CULINARY INSTITUTE,
MONTPELIER, VT

FRESH CRANBERRY SAUCE

Cranberries are popular all over North America. Fresh berries do have their season, but good quality frozen ones are always available. Cranberry sauce is traditional with turkey, but try it with ham or pork, too.

Preparation Time: 10 minutes
Cooking Time: 10 minutes
Serves: 4-6

INGREDIENTS

3 cups fresh or frozen whole cranberries
1 cup cane sugar
1 cup water

METHOD

Rinse and drain the fresh cranberries and pick over (omit rinsing if the berries are frozen). Mix the cup of sugar and water in a medium saucepan and heat gently until the sugar dissolves. Bring the mixture to the boil, stir and add the whole cranberries. Lower the heat immediately to a very slow boil. Cook the cranberries slowly, stirring occasionally, for about 10 minutes. Most of the berries will pop during this time. Take care not to burn. Remove from the heat and cool at room temperature in the saucepan or place in a heatproof bowl to cool. Refrigerate until ready to serve. Makes about 2 cups of fresh cranberry sauce.

NEW ENGLAND CULINARY INSTITUTE,
MONPELIER, VT

CHESTNUT STUFFING

Chestnuts make this bread stuffing rich and special. Dried chestnuts make it easy. Try the stuffing with game birds as well as with turkey and chicken for a pleasant change. If filling the bird with the stuffing mixture, do not fill until ready to roast.

Preparation Time: 20 minutes plus overnight soaking
Cooking Time: 1 hour and 10 minutes
Serves: 8

INGREDIENTS

8oz dry chestnuts
8oz dry white bread
1 quart warm water
2 tsps salt
2 cups chicken stock
2 tbsps butter
4 tbsps onion, finely chopped
4 tbsps celery, finely chopped
½ tsp black pepper
¼ tsp poultry seasoning
¼ tsp sage
1 large egg

METHOD

Cover the dry chestnuts with water and soak overnight. The next day, simmer the chestnuts in the soaking water for 2 hours until tender, but not mushy. Drain and cool the chestnuts, chop coarsely and set aside. Cube the bread and place in a large bowl. Soak in chicken stock and set aside. In a small skillet, sauté the onions and celery in the butter and add to the bread mixture. Add seasonings and stir in the egg. Add the chestnuts and mix well. Place the stuffing in a greased ovenproof pan, or use to fill a turkey, game bird or chicken. Cook in a moderately low oven for 1 hour.

NEW ENGLAND CULINARY INSTITUTE,
MONTPELIER, VT

VERMONT BAKED BEANS

What makes Vermont baked beans different from other versions? Maple syrup, of course! These beans take a long time to cook, but nothing this good ever came out of a can.

Preparation Time: 30 minutes plus overnight soaking
Cooking Time: 7-8 hours
Oven Temperature: 325°F
Serves: 8

INGREDIENTS

1 quart dried navy or yellow eye beans

4 slices bacon or ½lb piece salt pork
1 medium onion, chopped
½ cup Vermont maple syrup
1 tsp dry mustard
½ tsp ginger
¼ tsp pepper
1 tsp salt

METHOD

Pick over the beans, rinse with cold water and drain. Place the beans in a large pot and cover with about 4 quarts of cold water. Soak the beans overnight or at least 8 hours. After soaking, bring the pot of beans and water to the boil. Reduce the heat and simmer the beans about 1½ hours or until tender. Drain the beans and reserve the liquid. Place the beans in an ovenproof casserole or bean pot. Add the chopped onion and if using bacon, dice it before adding to the beans. Add reserved bean liquid to cover. Add the maple syrup and spices and mix thoroughly. If using salt pork instead of bacon, place on top of the beans. Bake the beans, covered, for 4-5 hours. Uncover, and cook another 3-4 hours, adding extra bean liquid, if necessary. May be prepared several days in advance and reheated.

NEW ENGLAND CULINARY INSTITUTE,
MONTPELIER, VT

THREE CABBAGES

Serve this dish with roast loin of pork for a combination that is popular in so many countries. In the true melting pot spirit of America, this recipe takes the sauerkraut of Germany, Savoy cabbage of England and red cabbage of Denmark and brings them together in one special dish. While the recipe is prepared in three separate sections, the cabbages are ultimately served together as one dish.

Preparation Time: 35 minutes
Cooking Time: 1½ hours
Serves: 6-8

INGREDIENTS

SAUERKRAUT

2 tbsps butter
1 medium onion, sliced
2lbs fresh sauerkraut (unrinsed)
1 cup white wine

6 juniper berries
6oz slab bacon
White pepper to taste

SAVOY CABBAGE

1 large Savoy cabbage, sliced thinly
3 tbsps butter
Salt and pepper

RED CABBAGE

1 large red cabbage, sliced thinly
1 cup red wine
½ cup red wine vinegar
1 tsp salt
¼ cup sugar
½ tsp thyme
½ cup water
¼ cup oil
1 onion, thinly sliced

METHOD

Melt the butter for the sauerkraut in a heavy saucepan and add the onion. Cook the onion slowly until it is transparent, not brown. Add the remaining ingredients and simmer 1 hour. Set aside.

Bring 2 gallons of water to the boiling point. Drop in the Savoy cabbage and cook for 2 minutes. Remove from the heat and cool immediately. Drain the cabbage well. Melt the butter and place in a bowl with the cooked Savoy cabbage. Toss, season and set aside.

Combine the red cabbage, wine, vinegar, salt, sugar, water and thyme and marinate the mixture in the refrigerator. Drain, reserving the liquid. In a heavy saucepan, heat the oil and sweat the onion slowly. Add the drained cabbage and stir. Add the reserved liquid and cook, covered, for 1½ hours. Remove the cover and cook the cabbage until the liquid is almost evaporated. Reheat the Savoy cabbage and arrange all three cabbages attractively together and serve with roast pork.

NEW ENGLAND CULINARY INSTITUTE,
MONTPELIER, VT

ROAST LOIN OF PORK

In early New England, pork was more plentiful than beef and the colonists frequently made use of this delicious meat. Pork loin used to be cooked with the crackling left on, as it is in England, but this is now out of fashion. Be sure to have the backbone and feather bone split to make carving easier.

Preparation Time: 20 minutes
Cooking Time: 40 minutes per lb
Oven Temperature: 450°F reduced to 325°F

INGREDIENTS

1 pork loin roast–2 ribs per person
3 large onions
Sage
Thyme
Salt and pepper

METHOD

Remove the roast from the refrigerator about 1 hour before cooking. Preheat the oven to 450°F. Rub the sage, thyme, salt and pepper onto all sides of the pork loin. Cover the ends of the bones with foil to protect them from burning. Slice the onions and place the pork on top of them in an ovenproof dish. Place the roast in the oven and reduce the heat to 325°F. Cook 40 minutes to the pound, basting often with the pan juices. Allow to rest for 15 minutes before carving. Accompany with Three Cabbages recipe.

NEW ENGLAND CULINARY INSTITUTE,
MONTPELIER, VT

UPSIDE-DOWN APPLE PIE

Many Vermont recipes have French counterparts and the origin of this one can be seen in the famous Tarte Tatin. When turned out, this pie looks so impressive you will be amazed that it was so easy to prepare.

Preparation Time: 25 minutes
Cooking Time: 40 minutes
Oven Temperature: 400°F
Serves: 6-8

INGREDIENTS

12 Golden Delicious apples
6-8oz butter
1 cup sugar
Rind of 1 lemon
Recipe for your favorite one-crust pastry

METHOD

Peel, seed and cut each apple into 6 wedges. In a frying pan, place 3-4oz butter and half the sugar. Cook on low heat, stirring occasionally, until the mixture reaches a light caramel color. Add the apples in small batches and cook until they are tender, but still holding their shape. Set aside and repeat with the remaining apples until all are cooked. In another small frying pan, place 3-4oz butter and melt until foaming. Add the remaining sugar and the lemon rind and cook until light caramel in color. Allow to cool. Pour the light caramel mixture into a large pie plate. Arrange the apple wedges side-by-side until the caramel is covered and all the apples are used. Make two layers of apples. Roll the dough and place on top of the apples. Trim the crust so that it comes to the edge of the apples. Bake for 40 minutes. Run a knife around the edge to loosen the crust and let the pie stand for 10 minutes. Place a large serving plate on top of the pan and invert the pie onto the serving dish. Serve with whipped cream.

NEW ENGLAND CULINARY INSTITUTE,
MONTPELIER, VT

CREAM OF PUMPKIN SOUP

There are more ways of using a pumpkin than just as a pie filling, and this soup is one of the nicest. For fun, use a hollowed out, well-cleaned pumpkin as a tureen to serve the soup.

Preparation Time: 25 minutes
Cooking Time: 20 minutes
Serves: 4-6

INGREDIENTS

4 tbsps butter
1 large onion, thinly sliced
1 pumpkin, 4-5lbs in weight
Nutmeg
Salt and pepper
1 cup heavy cream

METHOD

Wash and peel the pumpkin, remove the seeds and cut the flesh into cubes with a sharp knife. Set aside. Melt the butter in a large pot and add the onion. Sweat the onion slowly until

Previous pages: Three Cabbages, Roast Loin of Pork, Upside-Down Apple Pie and Lattice Apple Pie.
Facing page: Cream of Pumpkin Soup.

it is fairly tender. Add the pumpkin chunks and 1 quart of cold water. Season with salt and pepper and a pinch of nutmeg. Simmer for 20 minutes. Purée the pumpkin mixture in small batches, adding cream to each small batch. Return the soup to the rinsed out pot and reheat gently. Serve hot.

NEW ENGLAND CULINARY INSTITUTE,
MONTPELIER, VT

TRUITE AU BLEU

The French influence is at work in this recipe. It is, of course, only the skin of the trout which turns blue when cooked by this method. Success depends on using very fresh fish and minimal handling to preserve the natural slime on the fish skin.

Preparation Time: 30 minutes
Cooking Time: 40 minutes
Serves: 4

INGREDIENTS

4 live trout
24 live crawfish
⅓ cup red wine vinegar
1 small onion, peeled and sliced
1 small carrot, peeled and sliced
½ a lemon, sliced
2 sprigs fresh thyme
2 tsps salt
Melted butter for serving

METHOD

Combine all the ingredients except the fish and melted butter in a large pot and add 1 quart of water to make a court bouillon. Simmer for 30 minutes and allow to cool. Kill the trout by hitting it on the head once sharply with a heavy object. With a sharp knife, eviscerate the fish. Place the trout and crawfish into the court bouillon. Bring back to the boil and allow to simmer. Turn off the heat and let stand 10 minutes before removing the trout and crawfish to a heated platter for serving. Serve with melted butter.

NEW ENGLAND CULINARY INSTITUTE,
MONTPELIER, VT

Left: Truite au Bleu.

ACORN SQUASH WITH MAPLE AND PRUNES

Squash was one of the first vegetables the early settlers learned to grow. However, the many different varieties available now would have bewildered our forefathers. Acorn squash is a winter variety and the rind should be very hard for the vegetable to be good.

Preparation Time: 25 minutes
Cooking Time: 32-38 minutes
Oven Temperature: 325°F
Serves: 6

INGREDIENTS

3 medium acorn squash
12 pitted prunes
¾ cup Vermont maple syrup
3oz butter
Salt to taste

METHOD

Split the acorn squash horizontally with a sharp knife and remove the seeds. Blanch or parboil in salted water for 7-8 minutes. Remove the squash and place cavity side up in an ovenproof baking dish. Place 2 prunes in the cavity of the squash half, along with 2 tbsps of maple syrup, a pat of butter and a pinch of salt. Bake the squash in a preheated oven for 25-30 minutes, basting occasionally. Serve as a side dish with pork or poultry.

NEW ENGLAND CULINARY INSTITUTE,
MONTPELIER, VT

LATTICE APPLE PIE

The use of apple cider in this pie is characteristic of Vermont cooking. Taste the apples first to decide how much sugar to add and use white or light brown, as desired. Grating over some maple sugar is a delicious idea, too.

Preparation Time: 35 minutes
Cooking Time: 45 minutes
Oven Temperature: 450°F reducing to 350°F
Makes: 1 pie

INGREDIENTS

Use your favorite two-crust pastry recipe

FILLING

6 cups apples, peeled and thinly sliced
(Northern Spy apples are good)
1 tsp cinnamon
½ tsp nutmeg
1 tbsp butter
2 tbsps apple cider

METHOD

Line a 9-inch pie dish with half the pastry. It is not necessary to grease the pie dish since the pastry has a high fat content. Place a layer of apples on top of the pastry, scattering sugar and spices over. Repeat with the remaining apples and the sugar and spices until the dish is full. Dot the top layer with small pieces of butter and sprinkle on the apple cider. Moisten the edge of the bottom crust with a damp (not wet) pastry brush. For the top, roll out the remaining pastry and cut into strips. Place the strips on top of the apples in a criss-cross design. If a glaze is desired, brush with beaten egg mixed with a pinch of salt. Bake the pie for 15 minutes in a 450°F oven. Reduce the heat to 350°F and continue cooking for approximately 30 minutes longer, until the lattice is browned and the apples are tender.

NEW ENGLAND CULINARY INSTITUTE,
MONTPELIER, VT

MAPLE WALNUT BREAD

One whole cup of maple syrup gives a true Vermont taste to this quick bread. The orange juice adds a fresh tang. This bread is better if 'ripened' for at least one day before eating.

Preparation Time: 20 minutes
Cooking Time: 1 hour
Oven Temperature: 250°F
Makes: 1 loaf

INGREDIENTS

2 tbsps melted butter
1 cup Vermont maple syrup
1 egg, well beaten
Grated rind of 1 lemon
2½ cups flour

3 tsps baking powder
½ tsp baking soda
¼ tsp salt
¾ cup walnuts, chopped (3 reserved whole for decoration)
¾ cup orange juice

METHOD

Blend the butter, maple syrup, egg and lemon rind until creamy. In a separate bowl, sift the dry ingredients together and add the nuts. Combine the two mixtures alternately with the orange juice. Bake in a greased loaf pan in a moderate oven for 1 hour. After the bread cools, glaze with more maple syrup and put the reserved walnuts on top. Best served the day after baking.

NEW ENGLAND CULINARY INSTITUTE, MONTPELIER, VT

MAPLE MOUSSE

Refined from the sap of the sugar maple tree, maple is the finest of all syrups. Don't be tempted to use substitutes in this rich mousse; that would never be Vermont style!

Preparation Time: 30 minutes
Cooking Time: 10 minutes
Serves: 6

INGREDIENTS

6 egg yolks
1 cup Grade A Vermont maple syrup
1½ cups heavy cream

METHOD

In a saucepan, bring the maple syrup to the boiling point and cook rapidly to reduce from 1 cup to ¾ cup. Be careful not to let the syrup burn. Meanwhile, in a stainless steel bowl, whip the egg yolks until foamy. Pour in the reduced maple syrup slowly over the beaten egg yolks, whipping constantly. Continue whipping the mixture until cool. In a separate bowl, whip the heavy cream until stiff. Fold the cream gently into the mousse mixture and pour into a chilled bowl. Refrigerate until set and serve chilled.

NEW ENGLAND CULINARY INSTITUTE, MONTPELIER, VT

MAPLE BAKED APPLES

Maple syrup, for which Vermont is justly famous, finds its way into many of the state's outstanding recipes. Syrup in this recipe helps to make a delicious sauce for the baked apples.

Preparation Time: 5 minutes
Cooking Time: 35-40 minutes
Oven Temperature: 325°F
Serves: 6

INGREDIENTS

6 baking apples (Rome, Baldwin, Cortland, Greenings, McIntosh or Golden Delicious)
6oz unsalted butter
¾ cup Vermont maple syrup
¼ tsp mace
Juice of 1 lemon

METHOD

Wash and core the apples and place them in a lightly greased ovenproof dish. Combine the butter, maple syrup, mace and lemon juice in a saucepan and bring to the boil. Pour the mixture over the apples. Place the dish of apples in a preheated oven and bake for 35-40 minutes. Baste the apples often with the maple mixture. The apples are done when they soften and look shiny.

NEW ENGLAND CULINARY INSTITUTE, MONTPELIER, VT

POTATO PANCAKE

This is a great favorite for lunch with apple sauce and is also good as a side dish with braised meats. The coarse grating blade of a food processor can be used to prepare the potatoes more quickly.

Preparation Time: 20-25 minutes
Cooking Time: 10-11 minutes
Serves: 6

Overleaf: Maple Walnut Bread, Maple Mousse, Maple Baked Apples, and Acorn Squash with Maple and Prunes.

INGREDIENTS

3lbs chef potatoes (not baking variety)
1 cup clarified butter
Salt and pepper

METHOD

Wash and peel the potatoes. Using a mandoline or grater, cut the potatoes into shoestring pieces. Place one or two tablespoons of the butter into a small skillet (5 inches in diameter) on medium heat. Put enough of the shoestring potatoes to cover the bottom of the pan into the hot butter. Season to taste with salt and pepper. Cook the potatoes over medium heat, shaking the pan frequently so they do not stick to the bottom. Press the potato mixture down into the pan with a spoon or spatula, lower the heat and continue cooking slowly for 5-6 minutes. Flip the pancake over and finish cooking the other side for an extra 5 minutes. Remove from the pan and serve immediately or keep warm. Repeat the process until all the potato is used.

NEW ENGLAND CULINARY INSTITUTE,
MONTPELIER, VT

ROAST LEG OF VERMONT LAMB

Lamb has long been abundant in the United States, but it has frequently been neglected and badly prepared. Not so this recipe, which uses domestic lamb to its best advantage, simply prepared with rosemary to enhance the flavor.

Preparation Time: 30 minutes
Cooking Time: 20 minutes per pound
Oven Temperature: 325°F
Serves: 6-8

INGREDIENTS

1 5lb leg of Vermont lamb
Fresh or dried rosemary
Salt and pepper

Right: Roast Leg of Vermont Lamb, Potato Pancake and Baked Zucchini and Tomatoes.

METHOD

Remove the leg of lamb from the refrigerator 30 minutes before cooking. Pre-heat the oven and remove the outer white skin (fell) of the lamb with a sharp knife. Place the lamb fat side up on a rack in a roasting pan. Rub the lamb with rosemary, salt and pepper. Insert a meat thermometer, making sure not to touch the bone. Roast the lamb for 20 minutes to the pound or until the thermometer reaches the following temperatures: 155-160°F for rare; 175-180°F for well done. Let the roast lamb rest for 20 minutes before carving.

NEW ENGLAND CULINARY INSTITUTE,
MONTPELIER, VT

BAKED ZUCCHINI AND TOMATOES

Here is a taste of Provence from Vermont! It's a colorful dish, and a perfect way to use those bumper crops of tomatoes and zucchini in late summer. Serve hot or cold as a side dish or as a vegetarian main course.

Preparation Time: 25 minutes
Cooking Time: 20 minutes
Oven Temperature: 400°F
Serves: 6

INGREDIENTS

⅓ cup olive oil
2 medium onions, sliced
1 tbsp thyme
2 cloves garlic, chopped
6 medium tomatoes
6 zucchini

METHOD

Heat the olive oil in a saucepan. Add the sliced onion and cook slowly over low heat until golden brown. Add the thyme, garlic, salt and pepper to taste. Line the bottom of an ovenproof dish with the sautéed onions. Place the sliced tomatoes and zucchini over, overlapping the slices as shown. Sprinkle the top with a few drops of olive oil. Bake in a preheated oven for about 20 minutes.

NEW ENGLAND CULINARY INSTITUTE,
MONTPELIER, VT

CHANTERELLE OMELET

Chanterelles, those very French mushrooms, are also frequently found growing wild in wooded areas in Vermont. Avoid washing them, since they absorb water. Just wipe them with damp paper towels if cleaning is necessary. The omelet itself takes less than a minute to cook, so all the ingredients should be at hand before proceeding.

Preparation Time: 15 minutes
Cooking Time: 2-3 minutes
Serves: 1

INGREDIENTS

2 tbsps butter
3 eggs at room temperature
3oz fresh chanterelle mushrooms
2 tbsps finely chopped parsley
Salt and pepper

METHOD

Slice the mushrooms and melt 1 tbsp of the butter in a small pan. Sauté the mushrooms quickly, season with salt and pepper and add the chopped parsley. Set aside and keep them warm. Beat the eggs thoroughly with a fork or whisk in a small bowl. Place the remaining butter in an omelet pan and heat until foaming but not brown. Pour in the eggs and swirl over the bottom of the pan. Immediately stir the eggs with a fork to allow the uncooked mixture to fall to the bottom of the pan. When the mixture is creamily set on top, scatter over the sautéed chanterelles and roll the omelet in the pan by flipping about a third of it to the middle and then flipping it out onto a hot plate.

NEW ENGLAND CULINARY INSTITUTE,
MONTPELIER, VT

PUMPKIN CHEESECAKE

An interesting way of using pumpkin is to combine it with cream cheese in a deliciously rich cheesecake. Try it as an alternative to pumpkin pie for Thanksgiving dinner.

Facing page: Chanterelle Omelet.
Overleaf: Pumpkin Cheesecake.

Preparation Time: 20 minutes
Cooking Time: 1 hour 50 minutes
Oven Temperature: 325°F
Makes: 1 cake

INGREDIENTS

CHEESECAKE CRUST

1 cup graham cracker crumbs
¼ cup brown sugar
½ cup melted butter or margarine

PUMPKIN FILLING

4 8oz packages cream cheese, softened
1 cup granulated sugar
½ cup brown sugar, packed
5 eggs, beaten
2 cups canned pumpkin
2 tsps pumpkin pie spice
1 tsp vanilla

DECORATION

Whipped cream
Cherries
Walnuts
Fresh mint

METHOD

Combine the ingredients for the cheesecake crust and mix well. Press into a 9 inch spring-form pan and bake for 8-10 minutes at 425°F. Place the cream cheese in a mixing bowl and beat in the sugar until the mixture is light and fluffy. Add the beaten eggs gradually and mix in the remaining ingredients. Pour on top of the crust in the spring-form pan and lower the oven temperature to 325°F. Bake for 1 hour 20 minutes, or until the cake is firm around the edges. Turn off the heat and let the cake remain in the oven an additional 30 minutes. Cool on a rack completely before removing from the tin. Garnish the top with whipped cream, cherries, walnuts and fresh mint leaves.

BERNADETTE CHOUINARD,
DANVILLE, VT

SUCCOTASH

Succotash is an Indian name for a dish of corn and beans. Sometimes, the only beans used are lima beans. The addition of red peppers makes a trio of appetizing colors. Serve as a side dish with meat or poultry.

Preparation Time: 25 minutes
Cooking time: 15 minutes
Serves: 6

INGREDIENTS

2oz butter
2 cups cooked fresh kernel corn
2 cups cooked fresh lima beans
2 cups cooked fresh green beans
1 red pepper, seeded and thinly sliced
1 tsp salt
¼ tsp white pepper

METHOD

Melt the butter in a saucepan and add the cooked vegetables, salt and pepper to taste. Heat the succotash over low heat, tossing occasionally. Pour into a serving dish and decorate with the red pepper slices.

NEW ENGLAND CULINARY INSTITUTE,
MONTPELIER, VT

VERMONT COB-SMOKED HAM

Not all hams are the same. Cob smoking gives the Vermont ham a unique and very pleasant taste. Some Vermonters like to baste the ham with fresh apple cider during the last 30 minutes of cooking. Plan to serve 3 people with each 1lb of ham.

Preparation Time: 10 minutes
Cooking Time: 12 minutes per lb
Oven Temperature: 300°F
Serves: 3 people per lb

INGREDIENTS

1 Vermont cob-smoked ham
Fresh apple cider (optional)

Facing page: Succotash and Vermont Cob-Smoked Ham.

METHOD

Place the Vermont ham in a large roasting pan and insert a meat thermometer into the thickest part, avoiding the bone. Bake the ham, uncovered, for 12 minutes per lb. When done, the ham will have an internal temperature of 120°F.

NEW ENGLAND CULINARY INSTITUTE,
MONTPELIER, VT

PUMPKIN PIE

In the 18th century this pie would have been called a pudding. Spices were not included, though, until the clipper ships began their trade. In the Southern states, squash is often used as an alternative ingredient, but whichever you choose, Thanksgiving would not be the same without it.

Preparation Time: 25 minutes
Cooking Time: 45 minutes
Oven Temperature: 400°F
Makes: 1 pie

INGREDIENTS

1½ cups cooked and mashed pumpkin
2 eggs
1 cup milk
½ cup brown sugar
1 tsp cinnamon
½ tsp ginger
¼ tsp nutmeg
Recipe for one-crust pastry, baked until very pale brown

METHOD

Place all the ingredients, except the eggs and pastry, into the top of a double boiler. Over boiling water, bring the mixture just to the scalding point. In a bowl, beat the eggs until frothy. Stir a small amount of the hot mixture into the eggs and return the egg mixture to the rest of the hot pumpkin. Stir over heat continuously until the mixture begins to thicken. Pour into the baked pie shell. Bake the pumpkin pie until the filling

Right: Pumpkin Pie.

sets and a knife tip inserted into the center of the filling comes out clean, about 30 minutes. Serve slightly warm with whipped cream.

NEW ENGLAND CULINARY INSTITUTE,
MONTPELIER, VT

VENISON STEW

Vermont has more deer per land area than any other state, so hunting is popular and recipes for venison are abundant. In the 19th century, many French Canadians from Quebec settled in Vermont and their culinary influence is evident in dishes like this, reminiscent of French country stews.

Preparation Time: 30 minutes plus overnight
marinating
Cooking Time: 1½ hours
Serves: 6-8

INGREDIENTS

6lbs boneless venison shoulder, cubed
1 quart good quality red wine
¼ cup red wine vinegar
1 bay leaf
2 sprigs of fresh thyme
6 juniper berries
1 medium carrot, peeled and cut into ¼ inch dice
1 medium onion, peeled and cut into ¼ inch dice
2 celery sticks, cut into ¼ inch dice
4 cloves garlic, crushed
½ cup vegetable oil
½ cup flour
1lb mushrooms, quartered
1lb slab bacon, cut in ½ inch pieces
Pinch salt and pepper

METHOD

Combine the wine, vinegar, carrot, onion and celery and marinate with the cubed venison for 24 hours. Remove the meat and vegetables from the marinade and place in separate bowls. Reserve the marinade. Heat the oil in a heavy frying pan and brown the venison on all sides over high heat. Remove the venison from the frying pan to a large pot, repeat the browning process with the vegetables and add to the venison in a large pot. Sprinkle the flour over the combined meat and vegetables, stir and add the reserved marinade. Add salt and pepper to taste. Simmer for about 1 hour, remove the vegetables after that time and reserve them. Continue cooking the meat until tender, about 1½ hours. Meanwhile, blanch the bacon for 3 minutes in boiling water. Drain and sauté in the same skillet used for the venison. Add the bacon to the stew when the venison is tender. Sauté the mushrooms and add to the stew. Cook until all the ingredients are hot and serve immediately. A chesnut purée makes a nice accompaniment.

NEW ENGLAND CULINARY INSTITUTE,
MONTPELIER, VT

Facing page: Venison Stew.

NEW HAMPSHIRE

The essence of New Hampshire, some say, is expressed by the granite bedrock that underlies the soil, or by the stern rock profile in the Cannon Mountains known as the Old Man of the Mountain.

New Hampshire was one of the original thirteen colonies and, in typical fashion, started as a fishing and trading settlement. There is, and always has been, a spirit of fierce independence in New Hampshire. Armed resistance to the British occurred as early as 1774, when the rebel army seized Fort William and Mary, and the state even issued its own Declaration of Independence before the official one was drafted. Politics still play an important part in New Hampshire, for this is where the first presidential primary election is held.

The landscape of New Hampshire is quite varied. There are craggy peaks – the highest mountains in New England – extensive forest land with lots of game, and a beautiful coastline complete with sandy beaches, tidal pools, quiet coves, and marshy lowlands.

New Hampshire has much the same culinary roots as other New England states – Scottish, Irish, English, and French Canadian. Yankee tradition may still be strong, but New Hampshire's cooks like to experiment; they have taken many traditional dishes and given them style and panache.

In France, where choux pastry puffs originated, they are, more often than not, filled with a sweet mixture, but they are equally good stuffed with a savory filling, and, as New Hampshire people know, are especially tasty when that filling contains shrimp and cheese.

The French influence in cooking figures importantly in New Hampshire – as it does in most states near the Canadian border. Such dishes as Cranberry Duck l'Orange, Brace of Duck in Pears and Grand Marnier, and Chartreuse of Vegetables are all French in origin. With the former two recipes – each is delicious if prepared with New Hampshire's wild duck – the addition of fruit is a classic feature and helps to offset the richness of the meat. A chartreuse – a molded dish – is a culinary work of art. Consisting, by definition, of one main ingredient (in this case mashed potatoes), it is complemented by small quantities of choice ingredients – a colorful selection of vegetables. These are arranged in an attractive pattern, making this side dish so sophisticated that it can almost steal the scene from the main course!

New England Jambalaya is French in origin. This Cajun dish of seafood and rice was invented by the French-Canadians who settled in Louisiana. French-Canadians also immigrated to New Hampshire – hence the connection. This "northern" version of the dish features potatoes instead of rice, but since the essence of Cajun cooking is to use whatever ingredients are on hand, this adaption is not that strange after all.

Squash was one of the first vegetables settlers encountered in their new country, and it was cultivated in their first planting. Winter squash kept well, so people could store it for the long winter months when fresh food was unobtainable. A favorite recipe was a squash soup, which enabled the supply of this vegetable to go even further. The many varieties of squash added nutrition and flavor to meals.

New Hampshire's culinary repertoire is based on tradition, but demonstrates variety and ingenuity.

Facing page: New England Jambalaya.

GREGORY'S GOLDEN PUFFS WITH NEW HAMPSHIRE SHRIMP MOUSSE

Choux pastry puffs make elegant hors d'oeuvres. Shape them small to serve with drinks, or larger for a first course. New Hampshire shrimp and Cheddar cheese make these especially good.

Preparation Time: 25 minutes
Cooking Time: 40 minutes
Oven Temperature: 420°F reduced to 250°F
Makes: about 24 puffs

INGREDIENTS

PUFFS

1 cup water
4oz butter
1 cup bread flour
5 eggs

MOUSSE

1lb fresh cooked New Hampshire shrimp
4oz New Hampshire Cheddar cheese
2 tbsps minced fresh garlic
6oz farm fresh sour cream
½ tsp salt
½ tsp white pepper
½ tsp dry vermouth
½ tsp Helmet mustard, ground
1oz Danish blue cheese

METHOD

To prepare the puffs, bring the water and butter to the boil in a heavy pan. Once boiling, sift in the cup of flour and stir over very low heat with a whisk. Once the mixture comes away from the sides of the pan, beat in the eggs, one at a time. Continue beating in the eggs over low heat until the mixture is smooth and shiny—it may not be necessary to add all the eggs. Transfer the pastry into a pastry bag fitted with a large plain tip. Pipe the mixture out onto a greased baking sheet

Right: Cranberry Duck l'Orange, Red Bliss Potato Salad, Fresh Cranberry Bog Relish, and Gregory's Golden Puffs with New Hampshire Shrimp Mousse.

in amounts about 2 inches tall and equally wide. Alternatively, pipe out in decorative shapes such as little turbans or simple round mounds. Place in a preheated oven for 30 minutes. Reduce the heat to 250°F for 10 minutes longer, or until the puffs are golden brown and crisp. Remove from the oven and, using a sharp skewer, pierce a hole the size of a small plain piping tip in the bottom. Allow to cool completely while preparing the mousse.

In a food processor, combine all the mousse ingredients and blend until smooth. When the puffs are completely cold, fill a pastry bag fitted with a plain tip with the mousse mixture and pipe through the prepared holes in the puffs. Do not fill the puffs more than 30 minutes before serving.

GREGORY MARTIN,
WHITE RABBIT CATERING,
HOOKSETT, NH

CRANBERRY DUCK L'ORANGE

Indians were the first to use cranberries to brighten up food. The beautiful bright red color of these berries adds verve and their tangy, fresh taste is the perfect complement to the richness of duck.

Preparation Time: 20 minutes
Cooking Time: 1½ hours
Oven Temperature: 350°F
Serves: 2

INGREDIENTS

1 duck, about 4lbs in weight
1 tbsp ground sage
1 tbsp ground black pepper
1 tsp thyme
1 tsp nutmeg
Rind of 1 orange, grated
3 tbsps ground cranberries
2 tbsps olive oil
2 tbsps salt
3 tbsps orange juice

METHOD

Wash the duck and dry it well. Combine all the other ingredients and mix well. The cranberries can be ground in a food processor if desired. Rub the duck inside and outside with the mixture. Place seasoned duck on a rack in a deep

roasting pan. Line the pan with foil for easier clean-up. Cover the duck loosely with foil and roast in a preheated oven for 1½ hours, or until juices run clear when the thickest part of the thigh is pierced with a skewer. Serve with cranberry relish.

GREGORY MARTIN,
WHITE RABBIT CATERING,
HOOKSETT, NH

RED BLISS POTATO SALAD

Most of the goodness in a potato is in its skin. That is why potatoes, except if they are old and very thick-skinned, should not be peeled before they are cooked. Serve them in their skins too, whenever possible. Using red potatoes adds extra color and interest to the dish.

Preparation Time: 20 minutes
Cooking Time: 20-30 minutes
Serves: 8

INGREDIENTS

3 lbs Red Bliss potatoes
2 tbsps ground dill weed
1 tsp salt
1 tsp white pepper
1 tbsp chopped tarragon
12oz sour cream
1 tbsp parsley

METHOD

Wash the potatoes and cut them into 1-inch cubes. Place in salted water and cook until just tender. Remove from the heat, drain and allow to cool. When the potatoes are cold, toss with the remaining ingredients and serve chilled.

GREGORY MARTIN,
WHITE RABBIT CATERING,
HOOKSETT, NH

FRESH CRANBERRY BOG RELISH

Once the Pilgrims were introduced to cranberries, they made frequent use of them in sauces and relishes to accompany meats, poultry and game. The addition of lemon and lime in this relish adds a fresh twist to an old American classic.

Preparation Time: 5-10 minutes
Makes: about 4 cups

INGREDIENTS

2 cups fresh whole cranberries
2 cups granulated sugar
½ fresh lemon, cut into quarters
½ fresh orange, cut into quarters
½ fresh lime, cut into quarters
¼ tsp nutmeg
¼ tsp cinnamon

METHOD

Combine all the ingredients in a food processor to blend 2 minutes or until finely ground. Place in a saucepan and cook over medium heat for about 1 hour or until thick and bubbling. Stir frequently and add water if necessary to prevent drying out and burning. Serve with poultry, game, pork or ham.

GREGORY MARTIN,
WHITE RABBIT CATERING,
HOOKSETT, NH

BEAN SALAD WITH CAVIAR

This salad has a very European flavor. It may be served as a first course, part of a buffet of salads or as delicious accompaniment to grilled meat or poultry.

Preparation Time: 25 minutes
Serves: 6

INGREDIENTS

19oz can red kidney beans, drained
19oz can red cannelini beans, drained
3 cloves garlic, minced
5oz Swiss cheese, cut into small cubes
2oz black Icelandic caviar
¼ cup virgin olive oil
⅛ cup malt vinegar
1 tsp allspice
1 tsp white pepper
½ tsp Worcestershire sauce
1 tsp salt

METHOD

Drain the beans and combine with the remaining ingredients. Mix well, chill and serve.

GREGORY MARTIN,
WHITE RABBIT CATERING,
HOOKSETT, NH

GREGORY'S ROAST PRIME RIB OF BEEF BOUQUETIÈRE

This roast beef recipe is fit for a holiday feast or a lavish dinner party. The 'bouquet' of vegetables makes an attractive show. The shaped or turned vegetables mean that the carrots, potatoes and turnips will all cook in about the same length of time.

Preparation Time: 40 minutes
Cooking Time: 18-20 minutes per lb for the beef
5 minutes for the broccoli and cauliflower
15 minutes for the carrots, potatoes and turnips
Serves: 4

INGREDIENTS

1 4 Rib Roast of Beef, tied

SEASONING PASTE

2 tbsps white pepper
2 tsps salt
2 tsps Hungarian paprika
4 tbsps Worcestershire sauce

VEGETABLE BOUQUETIÈRE

¾ lb cherry tomatoes
¾ lb broccoli flowerets
¼ lb cauliflower flowerets
½ lb carrots, turned
⅓ lb potatoes, turned
⅓ lb turnip, turned

Overleaf: Gregory's Roast Prime Rib of Beef Bouquetière, Lively Poppy Seed Dressing, Fresh Green Native Spinach Salad, Bean Salad with Caviar, and Native Blue Hubbard Squash Soup.

METHOD

Mix the seasoning paste and rub over the meat. Place the meat fat side up in a roasting pan and cook in a preheated oven for 18-20 minutes per lb. Remove the foil for the last 30 minutes to allow the fat to brown. The meat is done when the internal temperature registers 145°F for rare. To prepare the vegetables, sauté the cherry tomatoes in 2 tbsps butter. Combine the carrots, potatoes and turnip, cover with cold salted water and bring to the boil. Cook for about 10 minutes and then add the broccoli and the cauliflower. Cook for a further 5 minutes, drain and keep warm. When the beef is cooked, arrange the vegetables around it to serve. Portion the beef equally, slicing one rib per person.

GREGORY MARTIN,
WHITE RABBIT CATERING,
HOOKSETT, NH

LIVELY POPPY SEED DRESSING

The sweet-sour flavor of the dressing is as perfect with a fresh spinach salad as it is with fruit or avocado salad. Make it well ahead of time to allow the flavors to blend.

Preparation Time: 5 minutes
Makes: approximately 1-1½ cups

INGREDIENTS

½ tsp mustard
2 fl oz white vinegar
1 tbsp poppy seeds
6 fl oz vegetable oil
2 tbsps sugar
Salt and pepper to taste
2oz onion, minced
1 egg

METHOD

Mince the onion in a blender and add the egg, sugar, mustard, vinegar and salt. Blend for 30 seconds. Add the oil gradually. Stop occasionally and scrape the sides. Blend again for 2 minutes and add the poppy seeds. Refrigerate until needed.

GREGORY MARTIN,
WHITE RABBIT CATERING,
HOOKSETT, NH

CHARTREUSE OF VEGETABLES

A chartreuse in French cooking is a molded dish that has one main ingredient complemented by smaller quantities of choicer ingredients, in this case, fluffy mashed potatoes with a selection of colorful garden vegetables. Be generous with the quantity of mashed potatoes because this is what holds the dish together. Don't be afraid to try it; it only *looks* complicated.

Preparation Time: 40 minutes
Cooking Time: 25 minutes
Oven Temperature: 425°F
Serves: 6-8

INGREDIENTS

Potatoes, peeled and cubed
Carrots, cut in julienne strips
String beans, trimmed
Peas
Zucchini
Summer squash
Cabbage leaves
Brussels sprouts
Cauliflower flowerets

METHOD

Cook the potatoes about 20 minutes and drain them well. Dry over heat while mashing. Trim the carrot sticks and string beans to fit the height of a soufflé dish. Slice the zucchini and summer squash, trim down thick ribs of the cabbage leaves and trim the ends of the Brussels sprouts. Parboil all the vegetables for about 2 minutes. Drain and rinse under cold water and leave to dry. Butter a soufflé dish thickly. Arrange a row of peas along the edge of the bottom of the dish. Next to the peas arrange a row of sliced zucchini and then fill in the center with circles of summer squash. Line the sides of the dish with carrot sticks and string beans, alternating the two. Butter will hold the vegetables in place. Carefully spread a layer of mashed potato over the bottom and up the sides to completely cover the carrots and beans. Add a thick layer to hold the vegetables together. Place a cabbage leaf or two on top of the potatoes and press gently

Facing page: Chartreuse of Vegetables.

to firm the vegetables. On the cabbage make a circle of Brussels sprouts around the outside edge and fill in the center with cauliflower. On top of that arrange another circle of zucchini and summer squash. Top with a cabbage leaf and fill with more mashed potatoes, smoothing the top. Bake in a preheated 425°F oven for 20 minutes. Remove from the oven and allow to set for 3-5 minutes before inverting onto a serving dish. If necessary, loosen the sides of the chartreuse from the dish with a sharp knife before turning out.

JAMES HALLER'S KITCHEN
PORTSMOUTH, NH

BRACE OF DUCK IN PEARS AND GRAND MARNIER

This dish is perfect for entertaining because it is impressive while being very easy to prepare. Fruit is always the perfect complement for the richness of duck and the mustard, Grand Marnier and honey add extra interest to the sauce. With New Hampshire's abundance of game, this sauce can also be used with wild duck.

Preparation Time: 20 minutes
Cooking Time: 50 minutes
Oven Temperature: 400°F
Serves: 4

INGREDIENTS

2 whole duck breasts cut from 6lb ducklings

SAUCE
2 ripe pears, peeled, cored and seeded
1 tsp mustard
1 cup Grand Marnier
1 cup honey

METHOD

Roast the two duck breasts in a hot oven for about 30 minutes. Meanwhile, prepare the sauce. Purée the pears with the mustard, Grand Marnier and honey. Simmer for about 20 minutes. When the duck has cooked for 30 minutes, drain

Left: Brace of Duck in Pears and Grand Marnier.

off the fat, place the duck breasts back in the pan and pour over the sauce. Lower the oven temperature to 400°F and bake for another 20 minutes. Skim any fat from the sauce and pour over the duck to serve.

JAMES HALLER'S KITCHEN
PORTSMOUTH, NH

FRESH GREEN NATIVE SPINACH SALAD

Use the youngest, freshest spinach possible. Be sure to wash it well and toss in a colander to remove excess water or use as a salad spinner. Serve as a light lunch or before an evening meal. Sesame seeds are fun sprinkled on top.

Preparation Time: 25 minutes
Serves: 4

INGREDIENTS

1 lb fresh garden New Hampshire spinach
¼ lb red onions, sliced
6 large mushrooms, sliced
4 cherry tomatoes, sliced in half
6oz poppy seed dressing (see recipe)
2 tbsps dried sesame seeds

METHOD

Clean, trim and wash the spinach well. Slice the spinach. Add some lemon juice to the mushrooms to keep them white. Arrange the spinach in a salad bowl and garnish with the vegetables. Pour over the dressing. Toss just before serving.

GREGORY MARTIN,
WHITE RABBIT CATERING,
HOOKSETT, NH

NEW HAMPSHIRE MAPLE BAKED BEANS WITH BOURBON

Baked beans are popular all over New England and each state has its own versions. The secret ingredients in this recipe are New Hampshire's own maple syrup, bourbon and, surprisingly, coffee.

Preparation Time: 15 minutes plus overnight soaking
Cooking Time: 9 hours
Oven Temperature: 250°F
Serves: 8-10

INGREDIENTS

1 cup pea beans (soaked overnight)
2 tsps dry mustard
½ tsp freshly ground pepper
¼ tsps ground ginger
3 tsps white vinegar
3 tsps malt vinegar
1½ cups strongly brewed coffee
¾ cup New Hampshire maple syrup
1¼ tsps dark molasses
1 large onion, finely chopped
¾ lb salt pork
¾ cup Jim Beam Kentucky Straight Bourbon

METHOD

Drain the beans and set aside. In a large bowl, combine mustard, pepper, ginger, vinegars and coffee. Add maple syrup and molasses and mix well. Add the onion and pork. Pour in the bourbon and stir in the beans. Transfer to an oven-proof baking dish, if necessary, and bake overnight (about 9 hours) in a preheated oven. It may be necessary to add water several times during cooking, so that the beans do not dry out.

GREGORY MARTIN,
WHITE RABBIT CATERING,
HOOKSETT, NH

NATIVE BLUE HUBBARD SQUASH SOUP

Naturally, the only blue thing about a Hubbard squash is its deep blue-green outer skin! The inside is a lovely golden yellow which lends a beautiful color to this soup. Because squash has such a mild flavor of its own, it benefits from the strong flavors of sherry and Worcestershire sauce and the dash of red hot pepper.

Facing page: New Hampshire Maple Baked Beans with Bourbon.

Preparation Time: 30 minutes
Cooking Time: 6 hours 30 minutes
Serves: 8-10

INGREDIENTS

1 cup water
3lbs blue Hubbard squash, peeled and cubed
½ cup roux blanc (equal portion of butter and flour
mixed to a paste)
2 cups lamb stock
1 cup chicken stock
3 tbsps dry sherry
½ tsp salt and pepper
½ tsp dried red hot pepper
1 tsp Worcestershire sauce
2 tbsps sweet butter
2 tbsps light cream per serving

METHOD

Combine the water and squash in a heavy saucepan and cook for 30 minutes, simmering gently. Purée the squash in a food processor and pour back into the saucepan. Add the other ingredients and stir well. Simmer gently for 6 hours, stirring frequently and adding more water or stock if the soup becomes too thick. Just before serving, swirl the cream into the hot soup.

GREGORY MARTIN,
WHITE RABBIT CATERING,
HOOKSETT, NH

CRUDITÉ VEGETABLE PRESENTATION WITH NEW HAMPSHIRE HORSERADISH AND GARLIC DIP

Raw vegetables with dips are easy to prepare and serve and they add a splash of color to an hors d'oeuvre selection. Using a cabbage to hold the dip is a whimsical touch, and you can eat the dish!

Right: Crudité Vegetable Presentation with New Hampshire Horseradish and Garlic Dip.

Preparation Time: 40 minutes plus overnight chilling
Serves: 8-10

INGREDIENTS

½ lb broccoli flowerets, washed
¼ lb cauliflower flowerets, washed
¼ lb julienne strips of carrot and celery
4 asparagus tips, cut into 3-inch lengths
4 radish rosettes
8 sprigs fresh parsley
1 head red kale or Savoy cabbage

DIP

6oz fresh dairy sour cream
1 tbsp minced fresh garlic
1 tbsp minced fresh horseradish
½ tsp white pepper
½ tsp sea salt
¼ tsp dry mustard
1 tsp cognac

METHOD

Blend all the dip ingredients together and chill 24 hours. Make the radish rosettes and clean and trim the vegetables. Hollow out a space in the cabbage deep enough to hold the dip, fill and place in the middle of an attractive serving dish. Arrange all the vegetables around the cabbage to serve.

GREGORY MARTIN,
WHITE RABBIT CATERING,
HOOKSETT, NH

NEW ENGLAND JAMBALAYA

Jambalaya is traditionally a Cajun dish, with its roots in Louisiana. It is normally based on rice with fish or meat or a combination of both. This New England version uses potatoes instead of rice, but it still has a lovely combination of fresh New Hampshire shellfish, ham and chicken, with a bit of chili pepper to spice it all up.

Preparation Time: 25 minutes
Cooking Time: 20-30 minutes

Facing page: Four-Layered Cheesecake.

Serves: 4-6

INGREDIENTS

2 cups diced potatoes
1 cup diced ham
1 cup diced raw chicken breast
1 cup chopped onions
1 cup dry sherry
2 cups water
½ lb each lobster, crab meat, scallops, shrimp and cod
Salt and pepper
½ tsp tarragon
1 chili pepper, seeded and finely chopped
1 quart light cream

METHOD

Place the potatoes, ham, chicken and chopped onions in a large pot and add the sherry and water. Bring to the boil and allow to simmer until the potatoes are cooked. Add the fish and shellfish and season with salt, pepper, tarragon and add the chili pepper. Stir well and add the cream. Cook over gentle heat until the fish and shellfish are cooked. Serve immediately.

JAMES HALLER'S KITCHEN
PORTSMOUTH, NH

FOUR-LAYERED CHEESECAKE

The chopped almonds and shredded coconut that form the base of this cheesecake make a delightful change from the graham cracker crust found on most cheesecakes. Also, this crust couldn't be simpler. Various flavors in the layers combine beautifully to make a cheesecake that tastes as good as it looks.

Preparation Time: 30 minutes
Cooking Time: 1 hour 55 minutes
Oven Temperature: 425°F reduced to 225°F
Makes: 1 10-inch cake

INGREDIENTS

½ cup butter, softened
¾ cup each of chopped almonds and shredded coconut

FILLING

3lbs cream cheese
4 eggs

½ cup flour
1 cup confectioners' sugar
½ cup dark bittersweet chocolate, melted
½ cup cognac
½ cup almond paste
½ cup Amaretto
½ cup praline paste
½ cup Frangelico
½ cup white chocolate, melted
2 tbsps vanilla
½ cup rum

METHOD

Grease the inside of a 10″ springform pan generously with the softened butter. Dust the pan with a mixture of almonds and coconut. Press the mixture against the butter to help it stick. Combine the cream cheese, eggs, flour and confectioners' sugar and beat until well mixed. Divide the mixture into quarters and add to one quarter the melted dark chocolate and the cognac. Pour this mixture into the pan on top of the crust. To the second quarter, add the almond paste and amaretto and mix well. Carefully spread across the first layer. To the third quarter, add the praline paste and Frangelico. Blend again and lightly spread on top of the last layer. To the final quarter, add the melted white chocolate, vanilla and rum. Pour this over the top and carefully spread out. Place in the oven at 425°F for 15 minutes; reduce to 225°F and bake for another hour and 45 minutes. Remove and allow to cool completely before refrigerating. Chill for 24 hours before serving. Decorate the top with chocolate leaves.

JAMES HALLER'S KITCHEN,
PORTSMOUTH, NH

SOUR CREAM APPLE PIE WITH CINNAMON

This is a pie with a most unusual pastry, tasting of cinnamon, maple and cider. That, and a filling of sour cream, Cheddar cheese and tart apples topped with a spicy sugar mixture which cooks to a caramel, adds up to an incredibly delicious dessert.

Preparation Time: 1 hour
Cooking Time: 55-60 minutes
Oven Temperature: 350°F
Makes: 1 9 inch pie

INGREDIENTS

CRUST
2⅔ cups flour
5 tbsps granulated sugar
¾ tsp salt
1¼ tsp ground cinnamon
6 tbsps butter, chilled
6 tbsps shortening, chilled
2 tbsps maple spread
4-5 tbsps chilled apple cider

FILLING
5-7 tart apples, unpeeled and cut into ½ inch wedges
½ cup shredded Cheddar cheese
⅔ cup sour cream
¼ cup heavy cream
½ cup granulated sugar
1 egg, slightly beaten
½ tsp salt
1½ tsps vanilla
3¼ tsps flour

TOPPING
3 tbsps grated lemon rind
3 tbsps brown sugar
3 tbsps granulated sugar
1½ tsps ground cinnamon
1 cup chopped walnuts

METHOD

Place all the ingredients for the pastry except, the apple cider, into the bowl of a food processor fitted with a steel blade and process for several minutes, or until the mixture resembles rolled oats. With motor running, pour in the apple cider until the dough clings to itself and forms a ball. Refrigerate for 1 hour. Roll out the dough between pieces of parchment paper and place in a greased 9″ pie plate. Combine all ingredients for the filling in a large bowl and mix until all the apples are coated. Add the apples to the pastry-lined pie plate and pour over any remaining mixture. Combine all ingredients for the topping and sprinkle over the pie filling. Bake on middle rack of a preheated oven for 55-60 minutes, or until the apples are tender and the filling is bubbling. Serve warm or cool.

GREGORY MARTIN, WHITE RABBIT CATERING,
HOOKSETT, NH

Facing page: Sour Cream Apple Pie with Cinnamon.

MAINE

Largest of the six New England states, Maine, the Pine Tree State, lies at the northeastern tip of the region. Originally forested by great stands of white pine, large parts of Maine still supply timber. Bordered by the Canadian provinces of New Brunswick to the east, Quebec to the northwest, and the state of New Hampshire to the west, Maine encompasses landscapes of rugged, picturesque beauty.

European settlement of the region dates back to 1604 and a short-lived French colony. The English, Scottish, and Irish followed, establishing more permanent settlements. French Arcadians, driven out of Nova Scotia, joined them, bringing their own, very different, ideas about food. The unfamiliar produce afforded by the New World led them to adapt their recipes. The heritage left by the Indians – staple crops such as corn, beans, and squash – quite simply saved the settlers' lives during the first difficult years, and, of course, the harvest of the sea was prolific, supporting the Indian saying that "Once the tide is out, the table is set."

Although measured in a straight line Maine's coastline extends for only 230 miles, its sawtoothed shoreline of deeply indented bays, coves, and inlets extends the total length to approximately 2,500 miles.

Together with the countless rivers, streams, and lakes, the state's waters provide a plentiful supply of fish and seafood, but none as tasty as its most famous inhabitant, the American or Northern lobster.

Fancy recipes such as Stuffed Lobster or Lobster Thermidor are heavenly to eat, but one of the best ways of enjoying this delicacy is to have it cooked at the water's edge on a summer evening. The Maine Shore Dinner is a true seafood feast for the eyes as well as the palate.

Piles of beautiful, crimson lobsters alongside sweet, delicate clams, called steamers, are positively irresistible. Maine clams are the soft-shell variety, dug by clammers on the coastal flats. Darker-shelled clams come from muddier flats, while lighter or whiter ones are from sand flats. While the clam season is year round, some flats are seasonally closed, or digging is limited, by local ordinance.

Everyone has his or her own idea about what to serve along with the lobsters and steamers. Some say the dinner needs no more than melted butter for dipping, while others like a fresh garden salad, corn on the cob in August, or fresh peas in July. Hot muffins, biscuits or rolls, potato chips, and vinegar for dipping all show up on various menus.

A clambake is something else again, although the ingredients are often the same. Once the lobsters and clams have been collected, a long pit is dug in the sand. A wood fire is laid and, when it's hot, rocks, coals, and more wood are added. After several hours all the wood is removed, leaving just the hot coals and rocks. A layer of seaweed is placed over the coals. Then, on go the lobsters, clams, and corn, wrapped in separate burlap bags, and another layer of seaweed. A potato in a knitted rope bag is placed on top and the whole pile is covered by a canvas. Why the potato? It's a natural timer. The potato turns out to be very important – when it is cooked, the seafood and corn are most likely done, too.

A story is told about an early colonist who, walking along the shore, came upon a group of Indians clustered around a large pile covered with a blanket. Clouds of aromatic steam, which the man found irresistible, rose from around the blanket. Not standing on ceremony, he tore off his jacket and plunged in to join the feast. That was the first Maine Shore Dinner, and the natives have been justifiably proud of their harvest of the sea ever since.

Facing page: Mouthwatering ingredients for a West Bay
Rotary Downeast Clambake.

DUCKTRAP RIVER SMOKED PLATTER

Ducktrap River Smoked Fish is flavored with brine, herbs and spices in combination with the savory smoke of northern fruitwoods. The Ducktrap Fish Farm in Lincolnville supplies some of the best smoked fish and seafood in the area.

Preparation Time: 15-20 minutes
Serves: 4 as an appetizer

INGREDIENTS

2oz smoked scallops
2oz smoked Maine shrimp
1 peppered mackerel

HORSERADISH SAUCE

1 cup mayonnaise
¾ cup sour cream
1 tbsps grated horseradish
Juice of a ¼ lemon

METHOD

Arrange smoked fish on a platter. Add saltine crackers and horseradish sauce. Garnish each serving with parsley and serve chilled.

THE LOBSTER POUND RESTAURANT,
LINCOLNVILLE BEACH, ME

WEST BAY ROTARY DOWNEAST CLAMBAKE

This style of cooking traces its origin back to the Indians. A colonist was said to be walking along the shore when he came upon several Indians grouped around a large pile covered with a blanket. Tantalizing clouds of steam seeped from the edges of the blanket, emitting a delightful aroma which the colonist found irresistible. He shouted in delight, tore off his jacket and joined the group to share their feast. Be sure to start preparations for your own feast at least 4 hours before serving.

Preparation Time: 1-2 hours
Cooking Time: 2 hours

INGREDIENTS

Lobsters
Clams or mussels
Corn-on-the-cob
Clam broth
Melted butter

METHOD

To prepare the pit, dig a hole in the sand about 1½ feet deep, 6 feet long and 3 feet wide. Fill the pit with wood and build a very hot fire. After about 1 hour, add granite-type rocks. Do not add shale rocks or rocks that hold water; they may explode. Place the rocks evenly over the wood and add coals. Add more wood if necessary, After about 2 hours remove all the burning wood leaving just the coals and rocks. To cook the seafood, place a 1-foot-thick layer of seaweed over the coals. Place the lobsters, clams or mussels and corn in separate burlap bags. Cover the bags with 1 foot more of seaweed. Place a potato on a knitted rope bag and place on top. Cover the entire pile with canvass. Cook for 2 hours. If the potato is cooked, the seafood and corn are done. Heat the clam broth and arrange with the cooked seafood, corn and melted butter.

RICHARD McLAUGHLIN,
THE LOBSTER POUND RESTAURANT,
LINCOLNVILLE BEACH, ME

NORTH ATLANTIC SALMON AMANDINE

Salmon, at its best, is said to be the king of fish. Traditionally, salmon was served in New England to celebrate the 4th July, but don't save a fish this good for once a year. Arranging the almond "scales" may seem like a daunting task, but for a special meal the effect is well worth the effort.

Preparation Time: 25 minutes
Cooking Time: 50 minutes
Oven Temperature: 350°F
Serves: 8

Facing page: North Atlantic Salmon Amandine. Overleaf: Ducktrap River Smoked Platter.

INGREDIENTS

5-6lb whole dressed salmon

STUFFING

6 cups crushed Ritz crackers
5 tbsps melted butter
¾ cup cream sherry
2 tsps salt
2 tsps Worcestershire sauce
2 drops red pepper sauce
1½lbs Maine crab meat

COURT BOUILLON

4 cups water
3 celery sticks, diced
1 quartered onion, stuck with whole cloves

GARNISH

1lb blanched, sliced almonds
1 egg white

METHOD

Remove the backbone from the salmon and combine with the court bouillon ingredients in a saucepan or a fish steamer. Bring to the boil and allow to simmer while preparing the stuffing. Combine all the stuffing ingredients and mix well. Spoon the stuffing into the cavity of the salmon. Rub the fish with melted butter and place in the top of the fish steamer or into a roasting pan. If using a roasting pan, carefully pour the cooled court bouillon over the fish. Cover with foil and steam in the oven for about 50 minutes. Remove the fish from the steamer or roasting pan and peel the skin from one side of the fish from the head to the tail, leaving the head and tail intact. Garnish the side of the fish with the almonds, using egg white to hold them in place, to give the fish a scale effect. Brown under a broiler until golden brown.

EXECUTIVE CHEF PETER McLAUGHLIN,
THE LOBSTER POUND RESTAURANT,
LINCOLNVILLE BEACH, ME

MAINE LOBSTER SALAD

Lobster salad is a luxury dish and the ultimate elegant salad. It is not a dish to economise on, so serve it lavishly. Traditionally, this salad is made with freshly cooked lobster, allowed to cool but never refrigerated.

Facing page: Maine Lobster Salad.

Preparation Time: 25 minutes
Cooking Time: 15 minutes
Serves: 4

INGREDIENTS

8 1¼lb live Maine lobsters
½lb salt
¾ cup heavy mayonnaise
4 large lettuce leaves

METHOD

Fill a 12 quart stock pot ⅔ full with water. Add ½lb salt (not a misprint) and bring to a rapid boil. Drop in the live lobsters and cover the pot. When the water begins to boil again, cook the lobsters for 15 minutes. Drain the water and allow the lobsters to cool . When the lobsters are cold, remove the claws and the small legs. Remove the meat with a nut pick. Twist the tail section completely around while holding onto the body. Break the ends off the tail (the flippers) and push the tail meat out. Pull the top strip of the tail meat back and remove the black intestinal tract, if present. The top part of the body shell can be pulled away exposing the tomally (the liver) and the body meat. All parts of the lobster are edible, with the exception of the shell, digestive tract and stomach. Cut the lobster meat into ¾ inch pieces, place in a mixing bowl and add the mayonnaise, stirring to just mix. Serve the lobster meat on crisp lettuce leaves. Garnish with parsley sprigs, if desired, and serve chilled.

EXECUTIVE CHEF PETER McLAUGHLIN,
THE LOBSTER POUND RESTAURANT,
LINCOLNVILLE BEACH, ME

MAINE SCALLOPS JARDINIERE

Beautifully cut garden vegetables in a cream and white wine sauce give a French flavor to the succulent scallops of the Maine coast. Buy the scallops with their roes, which are a great delicacy and, to preserve their round shape, cut them around the middle, if desired.

Facing page: Maine Scallops Jardiniere. Overleaf: Maine Lobster Stew – one of the state's many delicious lobster dishes.

Preparation Time: 25 minutes
Cooking Time: 20 minutes

INGREDIENTS

1lb sliced scallops
½ cup mushrooms
½ cup celery
½ cup carrots
2oz shallots, finely chopped
¼ cup dry white wine
1 pint heavy cream
Pinch salt and pepper
Small clove garlic, crushed
2 tbsps olive oil

METHOD

Cut the celery and carrot into thin julienne strips and blanch for 2 minutes in boiling salted water. Set them aside while heating the olive oil in a sauté pan. Sauté the scallops, mushrooms, shallots and garlic until the shallots are just transparent. Add the white wine and reduce by half over high heat. Add the cream and the remaining ingredients, and simmer until the sauce thickens slightly and becomes creamy. Garnish with parsley and serve over rice.

SOUS CHEF ROBERT KULIKOWSKI,
THE LOBSTER POUND RESTAURANT,
LINCOLNVILLE BEACH, ME

BOILED MAINE LOBSTER

The Maine lobster is the king of seafood and the main course in a Maine Shore Dinner. Greenish-blue when live, they turn bright red when gently steamed, sometimes over seaweed. Tender and sweet, they need no embellishments beyond melted butter for dipping.

Preparation Time: 15 minutes
Cooking Time: 10-15 minutes
Serves: 4

INGREDIENTS

4 1lb lobsters
Water
Salt
8oz butter, melted

METHOD

Fill a large kettle half full of salted water and bring to the boil. Place the live lobsters in the boiling water and bring to the boil for the second time. Cook the lobsters for 15 minutes. If cooking lobsters over 2lbs in weight, add 10-15 minutes to the cooking time. Serve the lobsters hot with melted butter.

THE LOBSTER POUND RESTAURANT,
LINCOLNVILLE BEACH, ME

BAKED STUFFED MAINE LOBSTER

Plain or fancy, Maine lobster is superb. This "dressed up" recipe has a luxurious stuffing of crab meat flavored with sherry. Wrapping the lobster in lettuce leaves for cooking keeps it moist and adds extra flavor as well.

Preparation Time: 30 minutes
Cooking Time: 20-25 minutes
Oven Temperature: 450°F
Serves: 2

INGREDIENTS

2-3lb Maine lobster
Lettuce leaves

CRAB MEAT STUFFING

4 cups Ritz crackers, crushed
4 tbsps melted butter
½ cup cream sherry
1 tsp salt
1½ tsps Worcestershire sauce
1 drop red pepper sauce
1lb Maine crab meat

GARNISH

Lemons
Parsley
Melted butter

METHOD

Combine all the crab meat stuffing ingredients. Place the live lobster upside down on a cutting board. With a sharp knife,

Left: Baked Stuffed Maine Lobster.

quickly split the lobster down the middle, being careful not to cut all the way through. Take the large claws off and remove 4-6 of the small legs and set aside. Spread the lobster apart and fill it with the crab meat stuffing. Put the lobster back together and completely cover the outside with lettuce leaves. Place in a preheated oven and cook for 20-25 minutes. If using a convection oven use the shorter cooking time. Remove the lobster from the oven, discard the lettuce leaves and arrange the small legs in an upside down V. Put the lobster under the broiler long enough to brown the stuffing. For best results, boil the claws in salted water while the lobster is cooking. Garnish with a fluted lemon half and parsley. Serve with melted butter.

EXECUTIVE CHEF PETER McLAUGHLIN,
THE LOBSTER POUND RESTAURANT,
LINCOLNVILLE BEACH, ME

MAINE STEAMED CLAMS

Maine clams are soft-shell clams and are delicious steamed, fried or in chowders. As part of a Maine Shore Dinner, they are often called steamers and are served in great piles alongside lobster and corn on the cob.

Preparation Time: 15 minutes
Cooking Time: 10 minutes
Serves: 7-8 clams per person

INGREDIENTS

7-8 medium sized soft-shell clams (steamers) per person
¼ cup water
8oz-1lb butter, melted

METHOD

Place the clams in a medium-sized kettle with the water. Cover and cook on medium heat until the clam juice (referred to in Maine as clam broth) boils up through the clams and all the clams are opened. Discard any that do not open. Serve them hot with melted butter and the clam broth. To eat, remove the tissue from the neck, dip the clam in the broth and then into the butter.

THE LOBSTER POUND RESTAURANT,
LINCOLNVILLE BEACH, ME

Left: New England Clam Chowder (left) and Maine Steamed Clams (right).

MAINE LOBSTER STEW

This is another and probably the most luxurious of the famous shellfish soup-stews from the East Coast. The dill pickles may seem an unusual choice as an accompaniment, but their piquancy is a perfect foil for the velvety richness of the stew.

Preparation Time: 30 minutes
Cooking Time: 1 hour
Serves: 8-10

I N G R E D I E N T S

4 quarts of whole milk
¼ cup heavy cream
¼ cup melted butter
1½ tsps Spanish paprika
3¼ lbs Maine lobster meat
(see Lobster Salad recipe for method)
Pinch salt

M E T H O D

Heat the milk and heavy cream in a double boiler. Do not allow to boil. In a heavy skillet (preferably cast iron), add melted butter and paprika. Heat slowly, mixing the paprika and the butter together to create a red butter sauce. Add the cold Maine lobster and heat slowly, turning the meat until warm, but do not over-heat. Add the warmed lobster meat to the hot milk and heat gently for at least an hour. Add a pinch of salt if necessary. For best results, remove the lobster stew from the heat and refrigerate overnight. Reheat the next day. Serve with oyster crackers, dill pickles and hot rolls.

EXECUTIVE CHEF PETER McLAUGHLIN,
THE LOBSTER POUND RESTAURANT,
LINCOLNVILLE BEACH, ME

NEW ENGLAND CLAM CHOWDER

There are many recipes for clam chowder because it is such a traditional and popular dish in New England. Some recipes include salt pork and some don't, but all are delicious. This one makes use of the prized soft-shell clams for which Maine is justly famous.

Preparation Time: 25 minutes
Cooking Time: 20-25 minutes

Serves: 5

I N G R E D I E N T S

3 quarts whole milk
5 medium-sized potatoes, cut in ¼-inch cubes
1 medium-sized Bermuda onion
6 lbs Maine soft-shell clams
1 tbsp clam base
½ tsp pepper
½ tsp salt
2 oz lightly salted butter

M E T H O D

Place the potatoes in cold salted water, bring to the boil and cook until tender but not mushy. Drain and set aside. Place the clams in a pot with ¼ cup salted water and cook until the natural clam juice boils up and the shells open. Set the clams aside to cool. Add the butter and onion to the pot and cook until the onions turn transparent. Add the milk and potatoes. Remove the clams from their shells and peel off the membrane. Cut the tip end of the neck off (the black part) and add the clams and their remaining ingredients to the butter and onion. Cook over gentle heat for about 1 hour. Excellent when reheated the next day. Serve with oyster crackers or saltines.

CHEF RICHARD A. McLAUGHLIN,
THE LOBSTER POUND RESTAURANT,
LINCOLNVILLE BEACH, ME

FRUIT MERINGUE CHANTILLY

During the 19th century in the United States, individual meringues were very popular and much enjoyed at teatime. Meringues are not difficult to make; just be sure that the whites are beaten to stiff peaks before any sugar is added.

Preparation Time: 30 minutes
Cooking Time: 1 hour
Oven Temperature: 275°F
Serves: 8-10

Facing page: Fruit Meringue Chantilly.

INGREDIENTS

Above: Maine Strawberry Shortcake.

1½ cups egg whites
¾ tsp cream of tartar
Pinch salt
2¼ cups granulated sugar
1 kiwi fruit, peeled
1 fresh pineapple, peeled and cored
¾ cup green seedless grapes
½ cup seeded purple grapes
3 navel oranges, peeled and segmented

1 banana, sliced and dipped in lemon or orange juice
3 cups heavy cream, whipped with ¾ cup powdered sugar
2 tsps vanilla extract
2 squares German sweet chocolate

M E T H O D

Let the egg whites warm to room temperature (1 hour). Beat the egg whites with the cream of tartar and a pinch of salt at a high speed. Once stiff peaks form, gradually beat in the granulated sugar, making sure the meringue mixture is stiff between each addition of sugar. Lightly grease and flour two baking sheets and drop the meringues with a spoon about 1¼ inches apart. Bake in a preheated oven for approximately 1 hour or until crisp. The meringues should stay pale in color. Remove to a wire rack to cool while preparing the fruit.

Cut the fruit into small pieces, leaving ⅓ in larger pieces for garnish. Fold the cut fruit into the whipped cream. Build the meringues in a tree formation using the fruit and cream mixture to hold the meringues together. Garnish with the remaining fruit and sprinkle with grated chocolate.

PATRICIA McLAUGHLIN,
THE LOBSTER POUND RESTAURANT,
LINCOLNVILLE BEACH, ME

MAINE STRAWBERRY SHORTCAKE

Few desserts say "summer" the way strawberry shortcake does. The biscuits can be baked in advance, and they also freeze very well. Shortcake is versatile as a dessert — serve it informally after a barbecue or arrange stylishly to follow a formal dinner.

Preparation Time: 30 minutes
Cooking Time: 10-12 minutes
Oven Temperature: 450°F
Serves: 6-8

I N G R E D I E N T S

BUTTERMILK BISCUITS

¾ cup plus 2 tbsps all-purpose flour
¼ tsp salt
1 tsp double acting baking powder
½ tsp sugar
¼ tsp baking soda
2 tbsps butter or margarine
¾ cup buttermilk

WHIPPED CREAM

4 cups whipping cream
1 cup powdered sugar
2 tsps pure vanilla extract

STRAWBERRY SAUCE

3 quarts strawberries
¼ cup granulated sugar

GARNISH

1 pint fresh strawberries, hulled

M E T H O D

Sift all the dry ingredients for the biscuits into a bowl. Cut in the butter or margarine until the mixture is the size of small peas. Add the buttermilk and lightly mix in. Turn the dough onto a floured surface and knead 10 times. Press out to a circle ¾ inch thick and cut with a floured biscuit cutter. Place on a baking sheet and dot each biscuit with butter. Bake in a preheated oven for 10-12 minutes or until risen and golden brown. Remove to a wire rack to cool.

Whip the cream until slightly thickened. Add the sugar and vanilla and whip until soft peaks form. Chill until ready to use.

To prepare the strawberry sauce, hull all the strawberries and place in a food processor with the granulated sugar. Blend until smooth. Strain if desired. To assemble the dessert, place half a biscuit on a dessert dish, cover with sauce and add a layer of whipped cream. Add the remaining half of the biscuit and top with sauce. Garnish each shortcake with more cream and fresh strawberries.

EXECUTIVE CHEF PETER McLAUGHLIN,
THE LOBSTER POUND RESTAURANT,
LINCOLNVILLE BEACH, ME

INDEX

ACKNOWLEDGMENTS

The publishers would like to thank all of the many individuals and organizations who so ably and efficiently prepared the food for photography, provided the expertise, recipes, food, cooking facilities, props, locations, advice and information. Without their invaluable assistance this book would not have been possible.

CONNECTICUT

Locations: The home of Arnold Copper, Stonington
The Cider Mill, Stonington
Recipes: Arnold Copper, Annette Miner, Daniel Routhier, Linda Routhier, Rita Routhier, Mary Roy and Margaret Thomas

MAINE

The Lobster Pound Restaurant, Lincolnville Beach, with special thanks to Exec. Chef Peter McLaughlin, Patricia McLaughlin, Assistant Chef Richard McLaughlin, Sous Chef Robert Kulikowski, Kitchen Manager Alan Feener
China provided by The Village Shops, Camden
Thanks also to Carl Sanford, Exec. Vice President of the Maine Restaurant Association

MASSACHUSETTS

Brooks Kelly of the Plymouth County Development Council, Inc. Stuart and Ruth Hall, The Mayflower Society Museum, Plymouth
The Sheraton Plymouth Inn & Conference Center for the supply of recipes and Chef Bobby Allan for their preparation
Photography at the cranberry bog by courtesy of John Talcot of the Federal Furnace Company
Props supplied by:
Cranberry Grapevine, Village Landing, Plymouth
The Dusty Miller, Village Landing, Plymouth

The Red Lion Inn, Stockbridge, Chef Steve Mongeon
The Village Inn, Lenox, Chef James E. Lowe
The Candlelight Inn, Lenox, Chef Marsha Heller
Union Oyster House, Boston, Chef Richard Kilums (Lobster Thermidor)
Hampshire House, Boston, Chef Neal Solomon
David Berger, Fine European Cakes

NEW HAMPSHIRE

Gregory Martin and staff of White Rabbit Catering, Hooksett

Blue Strawberry Restaurant
James Haller's Kitchen, Portsmouth

RHODE ISLAND

Interior pictures taken at the home of Steven Mack, Close Hill Farm
Additional recipes by Jack Felber, The Olympic Tea Room, Watch Hill
Hammersmith Farm, Ocean Drive, Newport
Recipes by Peter T. Crowley, La Forge Casino Restaurant, Newport

VERMONT

The publishers wish to thank Executive Chef Michel le Borgne, the instructors, staff and students of the New England Culinary Institute in Montpelier, Vermont, for their help in compiling this book. The Institute provided the recipes representing the State of Vermont, prepared and transported the dishes for the Vermont photographs, and assembled all the displayed native products. The publisher also wishes to thank the Cabot Farmers' Cooperative of Cabot, Vermont, for providing their Cheddar cheeses for inclusion herein; the Vermont Butter and Cheese Company of Brookfield, Vermont, for providing their cow's milk Creme Fraiche, and their goat's milk Fromage Blanc, Crottin and Tome cheeses; and the Guilford Cheese Company of Guilford, Vermont, for providing their Mont-Bert, Mont-Brie, Mont-Petit, Verd-Mont, and Mont-Arella cheeses. Also, the publishers thank William Barbour of the Vermont Wildcraft School in Barre, Vermont, for providing the Vermont chanterelle mushrooms pictured in this book, and Mr. and Mrs. Paul Chouinard of Danville, Vermont, for the use of their home and assistance in locating sites for other photographs.

Location and project co-ordination: Hanni Penrose